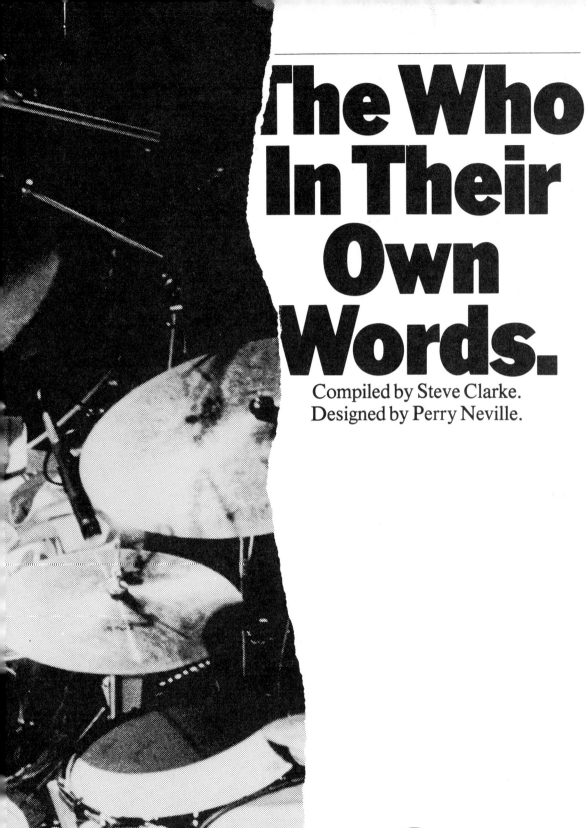

The Who In Their Own Words.

Compiled by Steve Clarke.
Designed by Perry Neville.

quick fox

New York/London

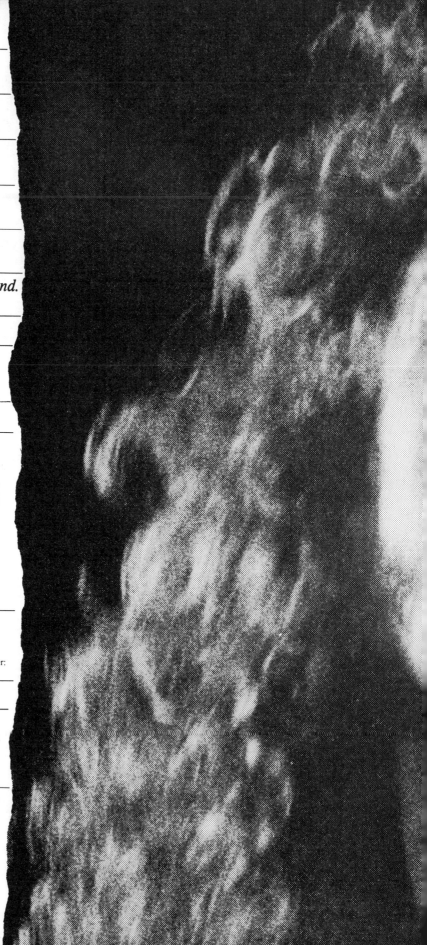

Published 1979 by Quick Fox
(a division of Music Sales Corporation)

Exclusive distributors:
Quick Fox, 33 West 60th Street,
New York, N.Y.10023, USA.
Book Sales Limited, 78 Newman Street,
London W1P 3LA.

Art Director: Pearce Marchbank.
Cover photograph: Colin Jones.

Thanks to Robert Ellis, Alexander Agor,
Colin Jones, Gary Herman, Pennie
Smith, Steve Mango, Matthew Taylor,
Brian Aris, Graham Hughes, David
Appleby, Michael Putland, Rex Features,
Camera Press, Syndication International,
London Features International, Keystone
Press, Pictorial Press, Music Library,
Robert Stigwood Group, MCA Records,
Polydor Records, Decca Records, Track
Records, Mrs. Moon, Mr. and Mrs.
Townshend, Mr. and Mrs. Daltrey and
Alison Entwistle for photographs used
throughout this book.
Thanks also to Chris Chappell and also
our apologies to anyone not credited here
who should have been.

Introduction © copyright 1979
Steve Clarke.

Typeset by DahDah Typesetters Limited,
Poland Street, London.
Printed in England by Lowe & Brydone
Printers Limited, Thetford, Norfolk.

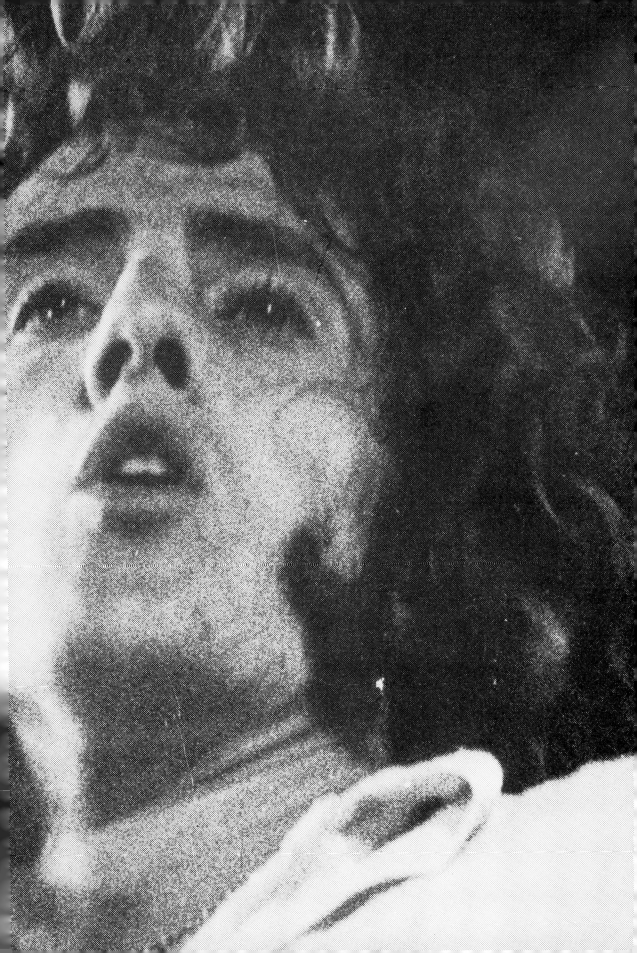

Throughout their fifteen year history The Who have been the most candid of the great rock groups. On occasion the outspokenness of a Daltrey or a Townshend has come close to ripping the group asunder, as one or the other of this volatile duo has vented his spleen. The Who have always washed their dirty linen in public.

Their willingness to be candid to the press, perhaps even their need to spill the beans to the public, surely stems from the very special relationship The Who has with its audience. No other act in rock comes close to rivalling the sense of rapport between The Who and their devotees. A successful Who gig is

6

not merely a coming together of the faithful, it's a heady trans-
cendental experience.

Townshend — arguably the best interview in rock — and his
cohorts feel a sense of responsibility to their audience which is
rare in so narcissistic a game as rock and roll. Unlike their peers,
the very individual individuals that are The Who have never been
far away from the public eye.

The Who In Their Own Words is then but a slice of all the
talking that's gone down between The Who and the press this past
decade and a half. Nevertheless, it is a segment which gives a truly
candid view of the most candid of rock groups. *Steve Clarke.*

The Story.

YOUNG KEITH MOON

KEITH MOON AS SEA SCOUT

Beginnings.

Keith Moon: At seventeen I got a job as a management trainee in a government-sponsored electronics firm. That was the first of twenty-three jobs I started within two years. I excelled at interviews. With my knowledge and personality I was always considered 'management material'.

John Entwistle: I had a choice when I left school of either going to art school or music school, but there was some trouble from my family about the music thing and I didn't particularly want to go to art school so I went into the tax office, where at least I was starting to earn money. I stayed there for about two and a half years, but all the time I was playing in a band for about five or six nights a week.

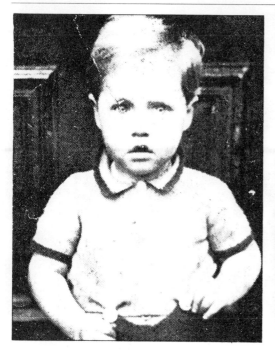

I was taught piano from the age of seven until the age of eleven. I was forced into it as my mother played piano, and from then on I convinced her that I should learn to play the trumpet and carry on teaching myself piano, which I

YOUNG ROGER DALTREY

never did, and then when I was fourteen I saved up some money and made myself a bass guitar. It was diabolical.

Roger Daltrey: I worked in a factory. I was an apprentice sheet metal worker for five years.

Roger Daltrey, on his first wife Jackie: I knew that if I didn't move away from her in those early days I would be a sheet metal worker forever.

Roger Daltrey: When I started, rock and roll represented a way out of the fucking gutter — a way I could be me doing what I wanted to do.

John Entwistle: If I'd never got into a group then most likely I wouldn't have started composing anyway. I'd probably be an amateur French horn player in an operatic society. I did a bit of everything — played Dixieland, modern jazz, brass band, military music — but most of my time I spent in an orchestra, Middlesex Schools' Orchestra. I played French horn in it for about two years. I really enjoyed that.

So he doesn't come from Shepherd's Bush?
No. I'm from Chiswick, which is a gnat's piss away. The reason The Who say they come from Shepherd's Bush is because that's the general circle we were moving around in when we first started playing. Roger lived in Shepherd's Bush and then moved to Chiswick so really it all came from the Chiswick, Ealing, Wembley area.

Pete Townshend: My father was essentially a pop musician in his day. I dread to think what

would have happened if I had been brought up in a classical family. He promised me a harmonica which I never got and in the end I think I had to shoplift one a couple of years later.

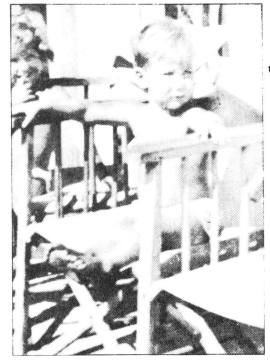

Pete Townshend: My granny got me my first guitar and it was a very, very, very bad one indeed though it cost her a lot of money. It's important to get a good instrument for kids. I fought tooth and nail with it for a year and finally gave up because it was too bad.

Keith Moon: I became involved in music through the local Sea Scouts band. I started out on trumpet, at which I was lousy, so one day I had a go at drums. I just picked up the sticks one day at headquarters and beat out a dance rhythm. I was amazed to find that I was a natural talent, that I did not need any formal training.

Pete Townshend: When I was at school the geezers that were snappy dressers and got chicks like years before I ever even thought they existed, would always like to talk about my nose. This seemed to be the biggest thing in my life; my fucking nose, man. Whenever my dad got drunk, he'd come up to me and say, "Look, son, you know looks aren't everything" and shit like this. He's getting drunk and he's ashamed of me because I've got a huge nose and he's trying to make me feel good. It was the reason I did everything. It's the reason I played guitar — because of my nose . . .

Pete Townshend: When I was a kid I had this enormous great hooter and I was always being

YOUNG PETE TOWNSHEND

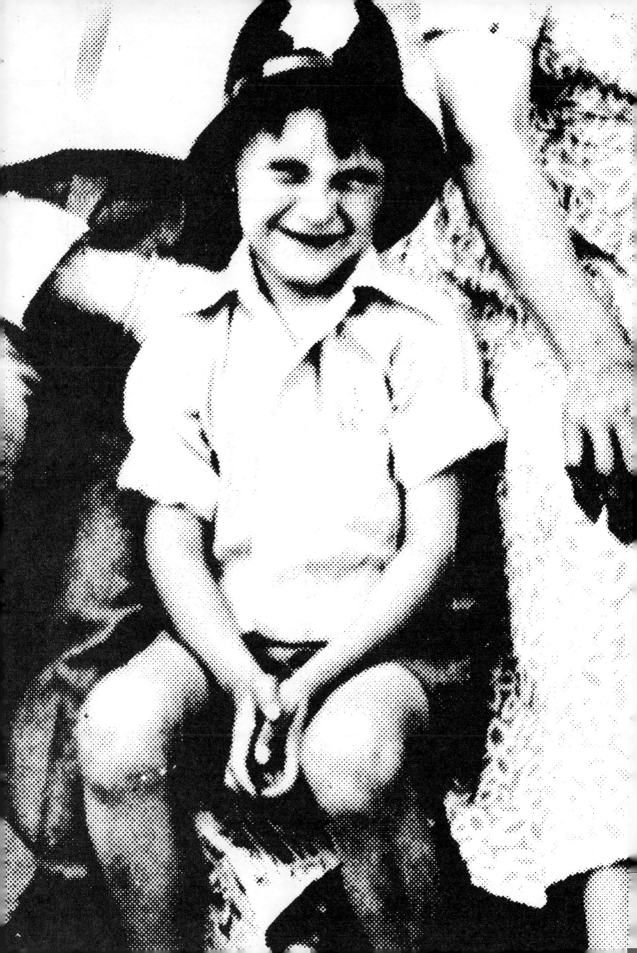

YOUNG JOHN ENTWISTLE

baited about it. So I used to think, "I'll bloody well show them. I'd push my huge hooter out at them from every newspaper in England — then they won't laugh at me." And when I first started singing with a group, I used to go up on stage and forget that I was Pete Townshend who wasn't a success with the ladies, and all of a sudden I'd become aware that there were little girls giggling and pointing at my nose. And I'd think, "Sod 'em – they're not gonna laugh at me!" And I'd get angrier still. My whole absurdly demonstrative stage act was worked out to turn myself into a body instead of a face. Most pop singers were pretty, but I wanted people to look at my body, and not to have to bother looking at my head if they didn't like the look of it.

Pete Townshend: John and I formed a group with two other boys from Acton County School. We played Shadows numbers, which must be the cliché story, but that's the way it was. There just weren't any other groups around. I was terribly happy with it, people quite liked us and it was incredibly exciting when we appeared in front of an audience.

   It gave me a new confidence — I hadn't made it very well with chicks and at the time when my mates started to get it together with chicks I was getting into the guitar and it became an obsession.

John Entwistle: I was at school, I was about thirteen and Pete and I were playing in a

Dixieland band. He played banjo and I played trumpet. When Pete took up guitar, about two years later, we formed another band. I'd built myself a bass guitar, Pete had an acoustic with a

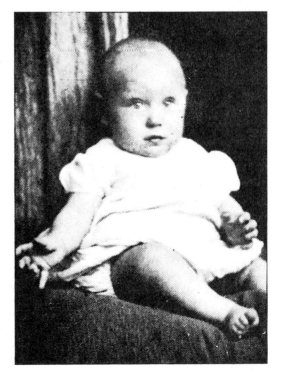

little pick-up on it, and we had a drummer and a vocalist who were in my form at school, and we did all the old Shadows stuff. We were getting nowhere fast, so I left and joined Roger's group. He was getting thirty bob a night playing firms' outings. He'd been expelled from our school, and I met him walking down the street one day and he said, "Here, can you play the bass guitar?" which was pretty obvious 'cause I was carrying one under me arm. He said, "Our group needs a bass guitarist, do you want to audition?"

The Detours.

Roger Daltrey: Well, all of us were like three loonies — Entwistle, Townshend and me. Always changing. We had quite a good following for a small local group. We were the first group to get fed up with playing the Top Twenty stuff, and move on to really hard R&B — like Howling Wolf and those sort of people. We were the sort of group that would always take chances on losing all the fans. The drummer we had was just like a . a . . . he didn't really fit in, in that sense. He wasn't a bad drummer, but Moony appeared one day and said, "I can play better than him" and he got up and within two minutes completely demolished his drum kit and we thought, "Christ, he's good. He's a loony!" So Moony joined.

Roger Daltrey: We went through about four lead singers and various people coming in with strange

instruments and then decided to sling everything out. There was another drummer at the time, so it was John, Pete, myself and this other drummer (Doug Sanden). We'd been through playing all pop music, it was just after The Beatles made it. We played Beatles songs for about six months and then we completely forgot that and went on a really heavy blues trip. That gave us our freedom, that's when we really started putting out any sort of new music . . . We went through this Johnny Kidd and The Pirates scene, copied everybody, you know, literally. That was The Detours, then we became The Who when we started playing blues and after about another six months we kicked the drummer out and Moon came along.

Keith Moon: First they were called The Detours, then The Who, then The High Numbers, then The Who again. I joined in the second phase, when they were changing from The Detours to The Who. I was in another group on the same pub circuit called The Beachcombers.

Keith Moon: I'd decided my talent as a drummer was wasted in a tight-knit harmony group like The Beachcombers and the only band that I heard of that sounded as loud as I did was The Detours. So when I heard their drummer had left, I laid plans to insinuate myself into the group. They were playing at a pub named The Oldfield. I went down there and they had a session drummer sitting in with them. I got up onstage and said, "Well I can do better than him." They said go ahead and I got behind this other guy's

drums, and I did one song 'Road Runner'. I'd had several drinks to get my courage up and when I got onstage I went *arrrrggghhhh* on the drums, broke the bass drum pedal and two skins and got off. I figured that was it. I was scared to death.

Afterwards I was sitting at the bar and Pete came over. He said, "You . . . come 'ere." I said, mild as you please, "Yesyes?" And Roger, who was the spokesman then, said, "what are you doing next Monday?" I said, "Nothing." I was working during the day selling plaster. He said, "You'll have to pack up work." I said, "All right, I'll pack up work." Roger said, "There's this gig on Monday. If you want to come we'll pick you up in the van." I said, "Right." They said they'd come by at seven. Nobody ever said, "You're in." They just said, "What're you doing Monday?"

Keith Moon: At the beginning I just couldn't get through to Pete and Roger. We really have absolutely nothing in common whatsoever, apart from music.

Pete Townshend, on his days at art college: There was a newness about art college, having beautiful girls around for the first time in my life, having all that music around me for the first time, and it was such a great period —with The Beatles and all that exploding all over the place. So it was very exciting . . .

Keith Moon: I don't really know whose name The Who was. I think it was a guy named Barney who was a friend of Pete's. And he said, "Well as you know, there's The Searchers, The Seekers, The Lookers, The Watchers, but let's have something abstract – Who! Yeah!"

Roger Daltrey: We got discovered by a Jewish door handle manufacturer. He decided he wanted

to waste some money on a pop group so we thought, "Well, we'll waste your money for you," which we did, with the greatest of pleasure. His name was Helmut Gordon. It was at the time everybody was exploiting any group . . . only The Who were a bit rougher than most. Then he got a deal together with Phillips and went in and recorded — we were going to do an original R&B number — that's when we got a guy called Peter Meaden — he was helping out — Helmut Gordon put up the money but Peter Meaden got the original ideas. That's when we latched on trying to be Mods. We recorded 'I'm The Face' and 'Zoot Suit' — Peter Meaden nicked the songs. He wrote the words to songs that were pinched from Slim Harpo. The original number was 'Got Love If You Want It'. So we threw the original words away — Meaden wrote some

words that were supposed to suit mods. It was hysterical. Horrible. I mean, I couldn't really get into it. I hated it. That fell through very quickly because it was such a bloomin' hash up. Then we met up with Lambert and Stamp (Kit Lambert and Chris Stamp).

They came up and saw us at a place called The Railway Hotel in Harrow, where we used to play every Tuesday. They'd been all around the country looking for groups. They saw us and went over the moon about us. They put us on a weekly wage — £20 a week each. Lambert and Stamp were both assistant film directors. Stamp was the brother of Terrence and Lambert was like first assistant.

Keith Moon on Kit Lambert and Chris Stamp:
We didn't like each other at first, really. They

PETER MEADEN

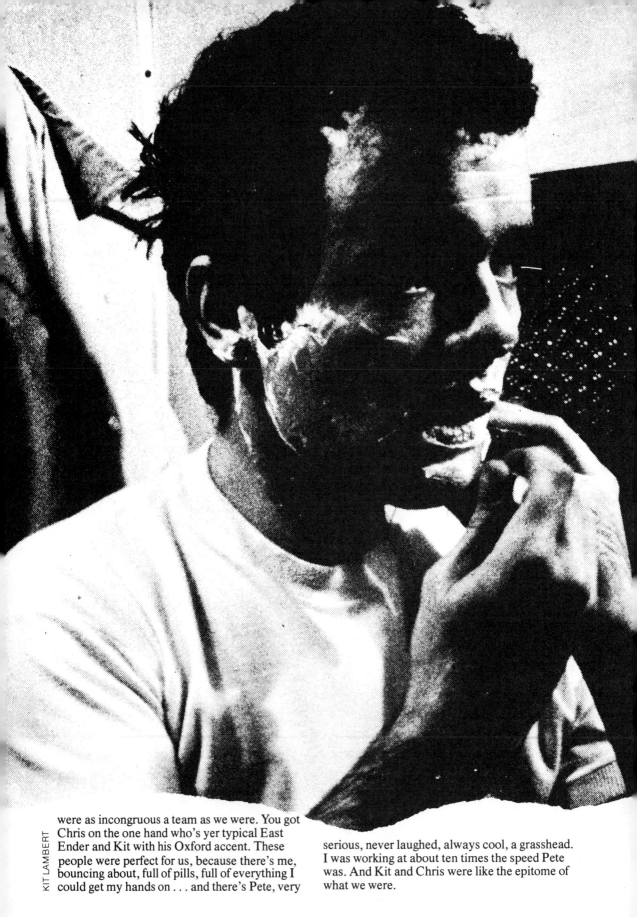

were as incongruous a team as we were. You got Chris on the one hand who's yer typical East Ender and Kit with his Oxford accent. These people were perfect for us, because there's me, bouncing about, full of pills, full of everything I could get my hands on . . . and there's Pete, very serious, never laughed, always cool, a grasshead. I was working at about ten times the speed Pete was. And Kit and Chris were like the epitome of what we were.

Pete Townshend: I heard 'You Really Got Me' on the radio and instantly I knew that The Kinks had filled the hole we wanted to fill. That sort of music always came from over the water. I thought that if you want the heavy stuff you could write it yourself. I wrote 'I Can't Explain' just for The Who and it remains one of the best things I've ever done. It was based on 'You Really Got Me'. It just didn't have the modulations. I was influenced more by The Kinks than any other group. Shel Talmy signed us and it was then I really got into writing. I felt I was intimidating the group by writing for them. I rowed Roger in on

CARD COLOUR
FOR THIS SESSION

R

VOX

THE WHO 1965

'Anyway, Anyhow, Anywhere' revising the lyrics, but that didn't really last. He started believing he'd actually written it. The next positive thing was 'My Generation' to show what was going on. It was as much a defiance to the group as a public thing. I felt I was the only person in the group that knew about dope. Keith was on pills, but I had heard about pot. I alienated myself from the group and this gave me

a pivot point to stand back and write and then join them in playing.

Lo and behold Lambert started producing our records. He spent incredible amounts of time with us and he changed my life fantastically. He'd listen to my demos and I'd make alterations. When we met I was the young drop-out and Lambert was the complete opposite, an ex-

28

public schoolboy and very respectable. Now we'd switched roles completely.

Roger Daltrey: We first started to get a really good reaction round the time we got our first residency at The Marquee in Wardour Street. It all escalated from there. It happened so fast, it was amazing. You had the feeling anything could happen. We were the kids' group.

Keith Moon, on smashing their instruments on stage: The way the story goes, Pete put the neck of his guitar through a low ceiling when he jumped too high, but that's not it. It happened when somebody got pissed off with the gig, with

the way things were going. When Pete smashed his guitar it was because he was pissed off. When I smashed my drums it was because I was pissed off. We were frustrated. You're working as hard as you can to get the fucking song across, to get that audience by the balls, to make it an event. When you've done all that, when you've worked your balls off and you've given the audience everything you can give, and they don't give anything back, that's when the fucking instruments go, because "You fucking bastards. We've worked our fucking balls off for you. And you've given us nothing back!"

That's one way the instruments got smashed. Another way was if a member of the group was too fucking stoned to give their best. Then he was letting down the other three. In a lot of cases it was me, through drinking too much. You know, just getting out of it at the wrong time. Then Pete or Roger or John says, "You cunt, you fucking let us down. You fucking bastard, if you want to get pissed, why don't you wait until after the show?"

Pete Townshend: If I can't get the sound I want out of a guitar I bang it against the amplifier. If I still can't get it, I drop it on the floor out of frustration. When I get the feed-back noise, it sounds like a bomber, so I put my own little flying to it, swinging my arms around; then, Moon can bang the drums and the audience thinks of guns and smashing people up. We're catering for their suppressed aggression.

Pete Townshend: I used to get terribly frustrated and compensate visually for what I didn't achieve as a musician. I tried to make playing the guitar look lethal.

Pete Townshend: We don't allow our instruments to stop us doing what we want. We smash our instruments, tear our clothes and wreck everything. The expense doesn't worry us because that would get between us and our music. If I stood on stage worrying about the price of a guitar, then I'm not really playing music. I'm getting involved in material values.

Pete Townshend: I like smashing things up. It gives me a release we all badly need. People in groups don't do anything these days; they roll up to the job, then do an hour on stage, then roll down to a pub or to a club. They do absolutely nothing — and I need a release.

Roger Daltrey: The whole thing about it was that we was doing something that *everybody* would love to have done — like buy a Rolls Royce and run it into a wall. What *is* an electric guitar? It's a plank of wood with a pick-up on it. Someone has the balls to charge three hundred quid for it. I mean, it's still a plank of wood.

Pete Townshend, on The Who as mod heroes: The mod image was forced on us. It was very dis-

MODS ON RAMPAGE IN MARGATE, EASTER WEEKEND, 1964

honest. The mod thing was Kit's idea. We were all sent down to a hairdresser, Robert James. Absolutely charming lad. We were then sent to Carnaby Street with more money than we'd ever seen in our lives before, like a hundred quid each. This was Swinging London. Most of our audience were mods, pill-heads like ourselves, you see. We weren't into clothes. We were into music. Kit thought we should identify more with our audience. Coats slashed five inches at the sides. Four wasn't enough. Six was too much. Five was just right. The trousers came three inches below the hip. It was our uniform.

We were playing a lot of Bo Diddley, Chuck Berry, Elmore James, B.B. King and they are maximum R&B. You can't get any better. Most of the songs we played were their songs. Pete

really got into his writing stride after 'Can't Explain'. Of course any song we did get hold of, we weren't playing straight from the record. We 'Who'd it', so that what came out was The Who, not a copy.

Roger Daltrey: We weren't ever mods. We weren't bleeding rockers either. I was never a mod.

Pete Townshend: I think The Small Faces were a mod group, and we were a mod group, and in their own way, I suppose The Stones were too, although they came from different sources and were quite old. We were a mod group because we picked the situation and went into it; the Stones were picked by the mods and dragged into it; and The Small Faces came out of the mods. We

weren't mods but we became mods, but had to learn all the stuff. I was at art college, had long hair, was smoking pot and going with girls with long red hair and all that. Painting farty pictures and carrying my portfolio around . . . and I had to learn how to become a mod.

Pete Townshend: What the mods taught us was how to lead by following. I mean, you'd look at the dance floor and see some bloke stop dancing the dance of the week and for some reason feel like doing some silly sort of step. And you'd notice some of the blokes around him looking out of the corners of their eyes and thinking "Is this the latest?" And on their own, without acknowledging the first fellow, a few of 'em would start dancing that way. And we'd be watching. By the time they looked up on the stage again, we'd be doing that dance and they'd think the original guy had been imitating us. And next week they'd come back and look to us for dances.

Roger Daltrey: We copied everybody. We were the original Japanese thinking group. You've got it, we'll copy it.

Pete Townshend: I figure that we will probably have about a year as a popular group. Could be less. Maybe more. But we want to make the most of the time we have. We would also like to get to No.1. I hope we make it with our next disc.

Pete Townshend: When I joined Roger was a very, very tough character. He stood no nonsense and if you didn't go his way you got his fist instead. If there had been a period when The Who might have split, it would have been in the days of 'My Generation'. We had an image of no time for anybody, and Mod arrogance, in a period when we were a very ordinary group. We hadn't really done anything good. We didn't have any self respect as a group, but we knew we were capable so we managed over a period to get it together, as they say.

Pete Townshend: I want to walk into a place and see this Conservative geezer standing at a bar all poshed up with a big car and I want to be just as well-dressed and have just as big a car, so that I can look at him and say, "Look at you! You're going bald!" And he won't be able to say anything back to me! I'm halfway there. I've got a flat in Belgravia and I like to spit out of the window if I feel like it.

Pete Townshend: We're scared of growing old. I personally wouldn't mind growing old in a Picasso sort of way or like Charlie Chaplin. But growing old, doing routine things after living a routine life really scares me.

Pete Townshend, referring to 'My Generation': Well, our next single is really pop-art. I wrote it with that intention. Not only is the number pop-art, the lyrics are 'young and rebellious'. It's anti-

middle class, anti-boss class and anti-young marrieds. I've nothing against these people really — just making a positive statement. The big social revolution that has taken place in the last five years is that youth, and not age, has become important. Their message is 'I'm important now I'm young, but I won't be when I'm over twenty-one.' Even London's streets are making a massive anti-establishment statement every Saturday night. This is what we are trying to do in our music, protest against 'showbiz stuff', clear the hit parade of stodge.

Pete Townshend: We stand for pop-art clothes, pop-art music and pop-art behaviour. This is what everybody seems to forget. We don't change offstage. We live pop art.

Roger Daltrey: What is pop-art? If it had come off . . . well you know. It started in a little way at the Marquee with us wearing badges and things. Unfortunately it backfired on us. It woke a lot of people up, but in the end it did us a lot of harm, especially with the press.

Pete Townshend: Kit used to brief us before we went into interviews about what to say; sometimes to be as objectionable, arrogant and nasty as possible. And oh, those outrageous lies we told! I remember telling Jonathan Aitken "I have got four cars, a Lincoln Continental, a Jag XK 150, a Cortina GT and a London taxi" – and all I had was an old banger. Then I said to somebody else that I was spending between £40 and £50 a week on clothes, and had to borrow money to go to Carnaby Street and buy a jacket in order to pose for a picture.

Pete Townshend: When we had a hit with 'Happy Jack', which was a very different sound for us, it became obvious that the musical direction of the group was going to change. I'd gone back to being influenced by The Stones again. On our second LP we really discovered The Who's music for the first time, that you could be funny on a record. Entwistle wrote for the first time. He wrote 'Whisky Man' and 'Boris The Spider'. My reign set aside as an individual from the group was over and the group was becoming a group. It was only then we started to work musically together.

Pete Townshend: We were all influenced and we openly admit it. I was influenced by 'Satisfaction' and by 'The Last Time' probably more than some of The Beatles' records — but I'm free to admit it. I'm part of the pop flow. The Who are part of the pop flow. And there will always be new groups to replace old groups — I don't know where they'll come from — but they will come. I've given up pointing an accusing finger at other groups because they have been influenced by The Who because I know I was influenced, and that everyone is, and that we are all part of one big thing.

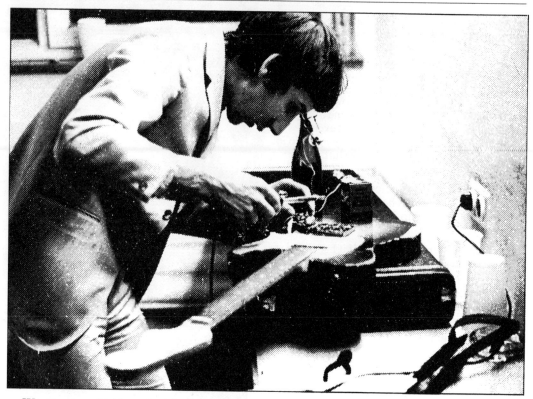

We came up with ideas, fresh ideas like the pop art clothes. We couldn't stand marketing Union Jack jackets. Someone else did. Someone else made money out of our ideas, but it doesn't matter. We might inspire some people, just like others inspire us. It's just a matter of being able to give and take and dig it.

Pete Townshend, on Townshend the guitarist: I couldn't find a model guitarist I could focus on. I used to like John Lee Hooker and Steve Cropper. I thought George Harrison was very tame. Keith Richard couldn't tune his guitar – he still can't. Somehow we became aware of The Yardbirds and we incorporated the things they were doing into our act without ever seeing them. It was done by word of mouth. I incorporated something into my style which Clapton hadn't discovered, this was feedback. I discovered it by accident because I wanted my amps to be bigger than I was, this was image consciousness again. I was the first person to put two Marshalls on top of one another and this, to my mind, originated the stack. Because the amps were directly opposite the stack, when I turned round I got feedback. After that I never looked at another guitarist and worried, I wasn't intimidated anymore. I was a guitarist and a songwriter and I could swing my arm, so I was confident.

Pete Townshend: Hendrix was the first man to walk all over my territory. I felt incredibly intimidated by that.

Roger Daltrey, on Woodstock: It was a nightmare. We got there at six and we didn't go on 'til six the next morning. It was murder — no food and no water.

Finances.

Roger Daltrey: When we got our first hit 'I Can't Explain' we started earning what was then pretty good money, say £300 a night. But after the first year we were £60,000 in debt. The next year, after working our balls off, we were still £40,000 down. And the biggest choke of all came one year after that when we found we were back up to £60,000 again. Every accountant's meeting was ridiculous. We always owed so much money that we ended up rolling around the office laughing ourselves silly.

John Entwistle: On the first American tour in 1967 when we were backing Herman's Hermits, we played thirty concerts and earned $40,000 – and I still had to borrow $100 to get home. It was heartbreaking.

John Entwistle: On our second US tour we worked from coast to coast, revisiting all the places we had done well at before. But the money just went. We even had $5,000 stolen from a bedroom. Then the biggest gig of all was cancelled because Martin Luther King was assassinated, and we came back after ten weeks with £300 each. There was a load of rubbish

ISLE OF WIGHT, 1969

talked at the time about the grand job British groups were doing in earning all these dollars. Really, we were being milked dry by the Americans. Why, I even remember one concert where the fellow actually fined us for playing too long.

Pete Townshend: Our debts were incurred in all kinds of ways — spending far too much on hotel bills, because in the early days we stayed in exactly the same kind of rooms as we do today — like a thirty dollar room and steaks everyday and a load of booze and a lot of guests and parties and things like that. But we were earning a lot less. That's the way we got accustomed to living in England and in Europe, and that's the way we

lived in America. We went into New York on the Murray The K Show and we stayed at the Drake Hotel. We spent five thousand dollars in four days at the hotel alone. We had to tip the man at the door two hundred and fifty dollars before they would let us have our baggage. That was the kind of world we were suddenly thrown into, and we couldn't figure the whole thing out. The bus bill. That seemed like a fundamentally good sense thing to do. It cost us about nine thousand dollars or something. There were incredible sort of money things going on. We tipped the bus driver a hundred, and he tore it up — because everybody really thought that we were earning millions and millions and millions of dollars. I

used to break a guitar every performance — if not two sometimes — and they would always cost around $150. They would always cost me an incredible amount of money to find – they'd cost like road manager's time and my time to look through pawn shops, local music stores and things like that. And Keith used to get through a lot of drum kits. He used to get a lot of stuff free, but you could never know, I mean just a set of skins for a drum set is about $300 and after every show he'd just go bang, bang, bang, bang, bang, through all the skins and then kick the whole thing over. I mean, literally — really literally — if 'Tommy' hadn't really sold a lot of copies we'd be exactly where we were then. And probably with a lot bigger problems, because our demands now equipment-wise are so much bigger.

Solo projects.

Pete Townshend: It's hard to explain, but it's a bit like you look up in space and there's the mother ship which is The Who proper, and all these little rocket ships that can go out and do very daring explorations, miles and miles away, deep deep into the universe, places where the mother ship would never go; and they discover new planets and get all kinds of experience, but they know that if they get lost someone will come back and save them and pull them back to the mother ship. I think it gives us more freedom, not less, as solo artists, and that is the funny paradox. I see people leave bands because they don't get enough freedom, and I think why the hell, they should have more.

Pete Townshend: 'Who Came First' wasn't really a solo album. In a sense, I don't think I've ever made one. 'Quadrophenia', if you like, was my solo album.

Roger Daltrey: I never acted before 'Tommy' in my life. I'll try anything once. I think if you're going to do anything you might as well do it at the deep end, and that's how I went into 'Tommy'. I went in head first and it worked.

Pete Townshend, on 'Rough Mix', the album he recorded with former Small Faces and Face Ronnie Lane: When it boils down to it, this is one thing this album is about, after ten years of the bloody rock business with its corruption, rip-offs, everything else. People fleecing us, stealing from us, screwing us, exploiting us, insulting us. After all that we get together, do an album, we enjoy it and it's good music. That's really all we care about.

John Entwistle: After my first solo album I really didn't think of any of my songs as Who songs. The only songs that they have used of mine since my solo albums started have been 'My Wife' and 'When I Was A Boy'. I started realizing there was no real outlet for my songs because The Who were more or less based on Pete's style of writing and Roger sang Pete's compositions best. I'd written my music for me to sing, really; I couldn't see Roger singing them. So I realized it was a choice — I was getting so frustrated that it was either leave the band or do a solo album.

Into the '70s.

Pete Townshend: The Who have moved up the rungs of the ladder of success at an incredibly slow rate. [1970]

Pete Townshend: The Who will probably last longer than most groups, but will never reach the status that these other groups have reached. [1970]

Crisis and disillusion.

Roger Daltrey: In many ways football has taken over from rock. There is more of the urgency stardom thing there. There is more competition, and the players know how to please their audience.

If they don't play well they get booed. It's not a complacent job, whereas for the past eighteen months, being a rock musician has been. The kids on the terraces really care about their team; they used to feel that way about their favourite group. [1972]

Roger Daltrey: I just don't feel I'm in a group unless we're playing on the road. It feels like you're just another session man. [1973]

Roger Daltrey: I think we take ourselves too seriously. I think the kids just come to see a good

rock and roll band which we were. And until we get back on the road, I say "were". I think that's where we should be. I hate being on the road but I love being on stage, and you can't have one without the other. The only part that's worth it is the two hours in front of the kids. [1973]

Roger Daltrey: We got drowned in synthesizers in 'Quadrophenia'. That was my main argument; you'll never get The Who to play like machines. We're not robots. It's down to us. If you want to add musicians, then it's not The Who. We've outlasted everyone because kids want to see The Who, these four people. You can't just turn it on

and off. Our audience wouldn't put up with it if The Who went on stage like Pink Floyd with an incredible light show and stood there like four dead people that sounded great.

Roger Daltrey: There's all sorts of problems going down at the moment that have got bugger all to do with the music side of it, which is usually lumped on my bloody shoulders. But I don't ever complain about it. [1975]

Roger Daltrey: The last thing I want to do is break The Who up. Anything I can do to stop that happening I'll do. I can accept the fact now that it's not going to go on forever. That's for sure. You do start to see the boundaries. But I just don't ever want to give up. The Who come before anything really. [1975]

Pete Townshend: It's just that when I'm standing up there on stage playing rock 'n' roll I often feel that I'm too old for it. When Roger speaks out about "We'll all be rockin' in our wheelchairs," he might be, but you won't catch me rockin' in no wheelchair. I don't think it's possible. I might be making music in a wheelchair — maybe even with The Who, but I feel that The Who have got to realise that the things we're gonna be singing and writing about are rapidly changing. There's

one very important thing that's got to be settled. The group as a whole has got to realize that The Who are not the same group they used to be. [1975]

Pete Townshend: I dunno what's happening sometimes. All I know is that when we last played Madison Square Garden I felt acute shades of nostalgia. All The Who freaks had crowded around the front of the stage and when I gazed out into the audience all I could see were those very same sad faces that I'd seen at every New York Who gig . . . It was like some bi-centennial celebration and they were there to share in the glory of it all. They hadn't come to watch The Who, but to let everyone know they were just original Who fans.

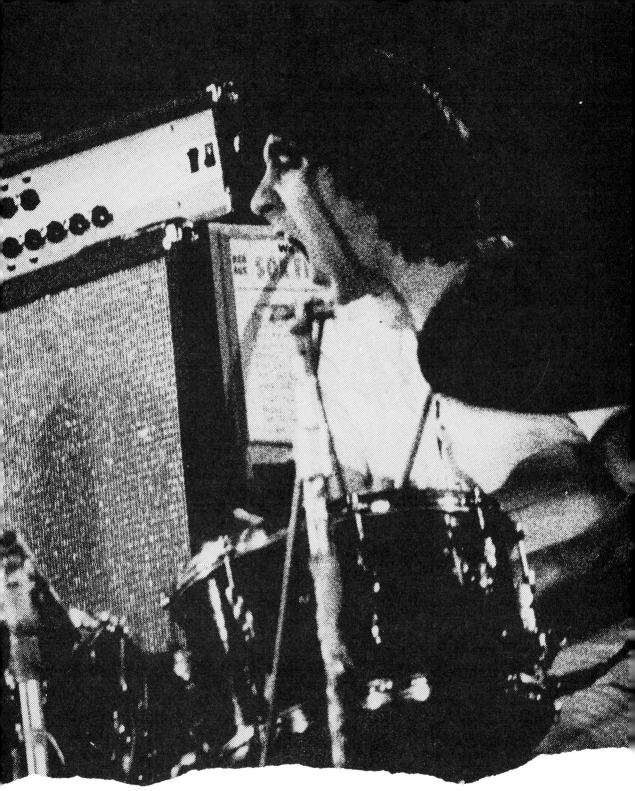

It was dreadful. They were telling us what to play. Every time I tried to make an announcement they all yelled out "Shhrruuppp Townshend and let Entwistle play 'Boris The Spider'," and if that wasn't bad enough, they'd all start chanting "Jump, jump, jump, jump." I was so brought down by it all. I mean, is this what it had all degenerated into? [1975]

Pete Townshend: The Who has been going for such a long time, and there's such a tremendous backlog . . . but for Christ's sake we haven't turned out that many records. If we'd been going for ten years and turned out records at the rate someone like Elton John does we'd have fifty albums to look back on. But it's still quite difficult to do a concert without having to go

through this thing of doing a representational flashback of the last ten years. You know, a quick summing up, and we're bringing you up to date with a few oldies but goldies, and a few of the medium, and then there was our Blue Period. And now we're going to do the John Entwistle spot where John plays for you John Entwistle fans a few of your favourite tracks. And now Keith Moon is going to do his comedy routine. And now, as frozen in the Woodstock film, Roger is going to put on his fringes as he sings 'See Me Feel Me' followed by, "everybody stand up please for 'Listening To You I Hear The Music'." It brought tears to my eyes really. It was tragic, absolutely fucking tragic, and I was the only one who could see it. I mean, to be fair, there were other people who could see it, but they couldn't understand why I couldn't soldier on . . . showbusiness. [1975]

John Entwistle: I wouldn't mind if we never released another single, ever. I hate releasing a poor little song to compete against football teams, comedians, wrestlers, one hit wonders. It's degrading. In fact, having a hit is extremely embarrassing! [1976]

Pete Townshend: I believe I've burned myself out, lived out my future in a sense. I still like the idea of performing because I've got an exhibitionist streak, but then I can always go down Studio 54. I think Mick Jagger will hold down his job a lot longer because his heart's still in it, that's the important thing.

I suppose I've been beaten down by life. It's a very intense experience on the road, in the rock business, and I don't for a second believe you have to behave badly or take drugs, but you can get carried away and you're encouraged to get carried away. Subsequently your values change. I think a lot of people in rock today are questioning their values and a lot of us are coming clean. I don't think I know why I was getting drunk and smashing up hotel rooms, and to be quite frank, never ever feeling guilty afterwards. But if I ever hurt a person — occasionally I've done it — that always weighed on me. [1978]

Pete Townshend: Electric guitar hurts my ears. It's bad to the extent that if I'm subjected to really loud noise for a long time, I get a lot of pain. And, apparently, pain is an indication of further damage. [1978]

Pete Townshend: The only time I feel the joy of rock and roll is when I'm actually on stage. But getting to the stage is another story; getting on a plane with Moon, going to an hotel, getting stuck in some dive in the States! Then you come back from a six-week stint feeling like a superhuman, but nobody around you recognises it, and you don't relate to your own family. What's *that* all about? It's just disorientation; unless you're

MOON AT PEPPERMINT PARK. ON THE NIGHT BEFORE HIS DEATH

gonna spend your life on the road until you die in an aircrash. Yeah, Lynyrd Skynyrd! I don't want to die in an aircrash! And I also don't wanna drink a bottle of brandy everyday, 'cause that'll kill me too. [1978]

Pete Townshend: We have to find another way to do shows if it's gonna fit in with being a young married with a couple of kids who're nine and seven and need to see me everyday. That's something I could never account for when I was nineteen and wrote 'Why don't you all fade away?' I never fuckin' knew one day I'd have two kids I missed with a physical pain when I was away from home. How do you deal with *that*? Big fucking rock star. [1978]

Pete Townshend: I think you should keep on playing rock for as long as you have an axe to grind and then if you haven't got an axe to grind you should go into cabaret.

Diversification and resolution.

Roger Daltrey: All the money we make from records is being poured into films. We are really hooked on movie-making. That's why we bought a £350,000 stake in Shepperton Studios.

Pete Townshend: We feel that whatever we do in the future — whether we tour, make records, make films, become perpetual businessmen — we would

continue to work together in one way or another. In fact, it's been a bloody hard job keeping the band together, and there has been a point when it would have been easy just to walk away. But we didn't. So we're now determined to reap the benefits of one another's company, friendship and joint experience.

Roger Daltrey: The Who have always been the one family in the street that fucks up the neighbourhood. And there's a weird thing happening at the moment. We're suddenly finding great, great joy in realizing that in essence we're all very much the same.

Keith Moon's death.

Roger Daltrey: The Who as it was, is finished . . . dead and gone with Keith. There is no question of us simply finding another drummer because it can't be done. It wouldn't be the same. Keith was the best drummer in the world. A hundred others couldn't replace him.

John Entwistle: I don't have to worry so much about the drums now. Keith was so unpredictable . . . . I used to worry if he would go out of time. Kenny is a lot more consistent, and he's a lot easier to play with. Keith was the hardest drummer in the world to play with.

Pete Townshend: Keith's death made us think very carefully. All of us felt that if we had been on the road working that day we would have walked

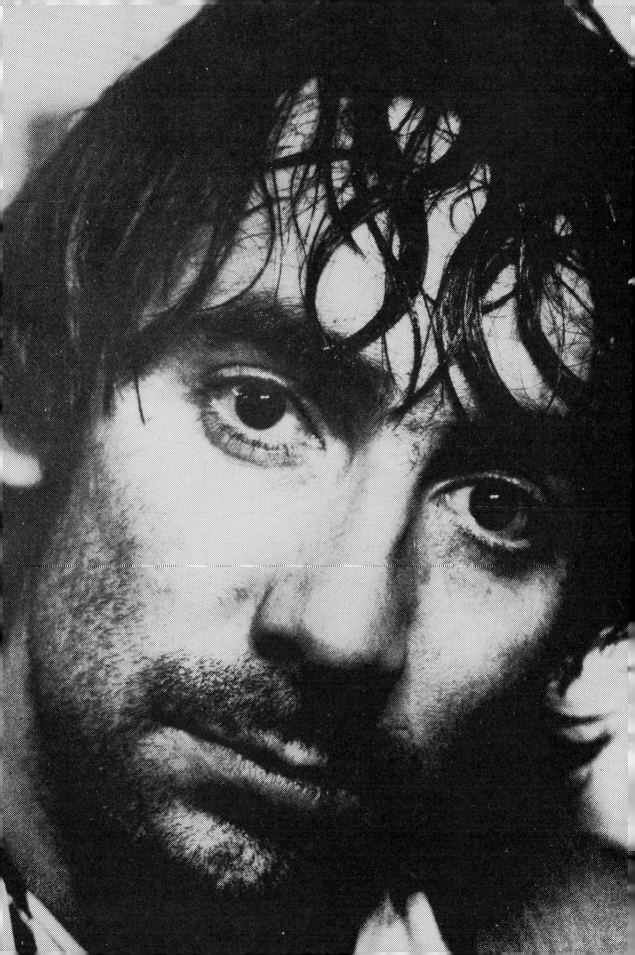

him up and down like we had done a dozen times before, and he would have recovered. It prompted us to realise that it could just as easily have been any one of us. The Who were sleepwalking along the edge of a cliff, the band had become a celebration of itself and was slowly grinding to a halt. But no one would take a decision to call it a day. It's made me think very hard. I decided to become more involved again. To get out and work.

Pete Townshend: We're no longer cardboard cut-outs of The Who. Keith's death put a stop to that. The Who are at risk and our reputation is on the line. We can't take anything for granted. The days of being able to sell out every night at the Empire Pool, Wembley, for six months are gone. A couple of really bad concerts and an armful of adverse reviews and The Who could be finished. I find that tremendously exciting.

Pete Townshend: I really broke down when we first went into the studio and he wasn't there. But I don't think anyone in the band has got any idea of what it will be like to get up on stage, and find that Keith's not behind them.

Roger Daltrey: The Who aren't as funny any more.

Pete Townshend, on Kenny Jones, late of The Small Faces and The Faces, who 'replaced' Moon in late 1978: It can never be as good without Keith, but we want to go on. Kenny was our first and only choice. He fits in perfectly.

Pete Townshend: What The Who are trying to do is exist in England — which isn't easy at the moment — and take care of the responsibility to allow rock to mature and do it without crapping over everything. If we can do just that and still remain human beings at the other end of it then I honestly believe we've achieved one helluva lot.

We've lost one of our members so far and it's a painful loss . . . something that we never ever thought would happen to us. We thought we would survive, but one cannot deny the fact that rock'n'roll has claimed so many young people. Maybe the statistics would be the same if you ran a survey on any other stress profession, but the fact remains that losing Keith was a terrible shock.

Kenny Jones: I still feel a bit weird about joining The Who, because Keith is dead. If Keith had left the band, and then they asked me, I'd be fine. But Keith is gone and I miss him.

The Songs.

Songwriting.

Roger Daltrey: Nothing would please me more than to be able to write songs, but unfortunately I'm not a songwriter. Believe me, if anybody's tried, I have. I'm not a natural. I'm just pleased that I can give Pete's songs the airings that he wants them to have, and I think I sing them better than anyone he could pick to sing them, and I'm pleased about that. If I can't have everything, I've got that at least.

Pete Townshend: Compositions come out so fast in rock because there's a demand created and contracts have to be fulfilled. I mean, whoever put Beethoven under contract?

Pete Townshend: You can only write about fairly unsubtle emotions. You normally have to write about adolescent emotions and feelings, about frustration or about unsaid, undiscovered and undone territory. It (rock music) can't break out of its limitations; it can't break out of being a mixture of light entertainment, dance music and a bit of thought on the side – it can't really be much more than that. But it can be a chunk of time, a chunk of history.

'I Can't Explain'

Pete Townshend: I wrote 'I Can't Explain' about a kid who couldn't explain to a girl that he loved her – that was all it was about, 'I fink it's love but I can't explain.' A couple of months later it was on the charts, and I started to look at it closely – because I was no fool, I tell you that — and I realised that the song was on the chart not because it was a little love song, but because it openly paraded a sort of weakness.

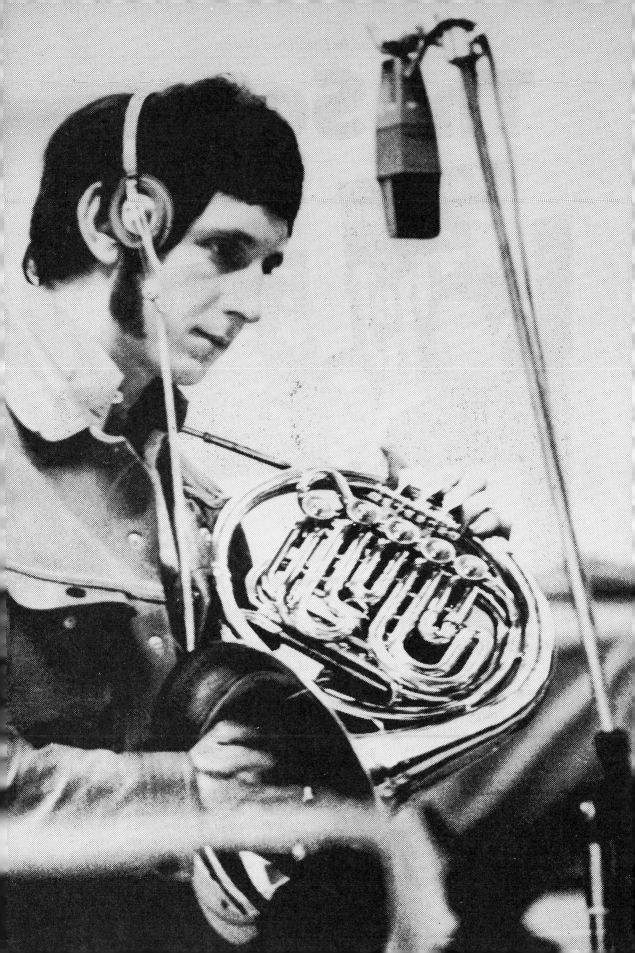

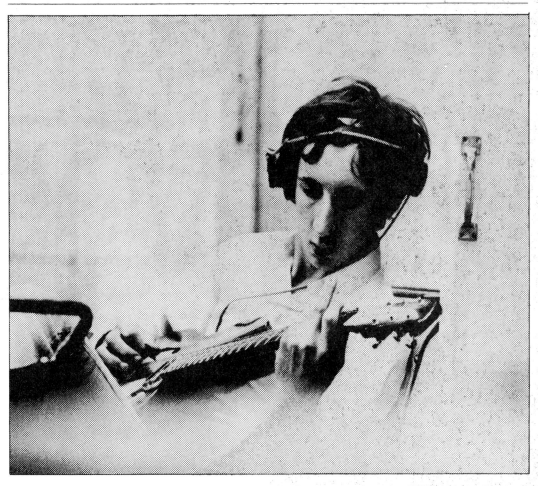

'My Generation'

Pete Townshend: 'My Generation' was written under pressure. Someone said, "Make a statement, make a statement, make a statement" and I'm going, "Okay, okay, okay." And I got 'My Generation' together very quickly, like in a night — it feels like that. It's a very blustering kind of blurting thing. A lot of our early records were. 'I Can't Explain' was a blurter and a bluster, and 'Anyway, Anyhow, Anywhere', which was our second record, was just a brag, like you know, nothing more. 'Substitute' was a take-off on Mick Jagger or something equally banal.

Roger Daltrey: The song just tells about a young lad who's trying to express himself, you know — apart from that, it was freezing in the studios when we recorded it. That's why I stutter on the lyric.

Keith Moon: Pete had written out the words and gave them to Roger in the studio. He'd never seen them before, he was unfamiliar with the words, so when he read them through the first time, he stuttered. Kit was producing us then and when Roger stuttered, Kit said, "We leave it in;

we leave in the stuttering." When we realised what happened, it knocked us all sideways. And it happened simply because Roger couldn't read the words.

Pete Townshend: It's a very big social comment. It's the only really successful social comment I've ever made — some pilled-up mod dancing around, trying to explain to you why he's such a groovy guy, but he can't because he's so stoned he can hardly talk. People saw different aspects of the record. It was repetitive, there were lots of effective key changes in it so it didn't bore you too much. And there was a bit of feedback at the end to keep people happy. It was our biggest seller and we never hope or want to produce anything like it again. [1967]

Pete Townshend: When I wrote 'My Generation' I condemned everybody except my own generation and I rapidly found out that most of my own generation were wasters and very eager to get on the dole. All they wanted to do was prop up the bar at the pub. I was very glad when I got away from it. Now I think that behind every bar propper-up and every geezer on the dole is a desperate man. That's really what

'Quadrophenia' was all about, that you could take a kid, who had everything going for him, an explosive individual, and you could squash him down. They end up not wanting to change society anymore but make their own immediate life a bit better, or ever quieter.

Pete Townshend: The story in 'My Generation' is about someone trying to object about today's poor educational system but can't get it out because he stammers. I suppose it will be called protest, but I hope not because I think protest songs are a load of rubbish. I don't really think much about the troubles outside this country, you know, Oxfam and all that. In this country our biggest worry must be the educational system. Take people here under nineteen. I haven't yet met many who've had an education like myself. I went to an ordinary grammar school. The present school set-up is all wrong. British education lacks

uniformity. You go to a grammar school now and are told that you have two choices of diplomas to study for. How is anyone of around fifteen or sixteen years old expected to be able to choose which one to take? They get confused.

Roger Daltrey: Every song Pete writes he produces for us as a demonstration disc. He makes them himself at home — accompanying himself on guitar, then adding a second guitar track or maybe bass, and then filling in with drums. Then he sends each of us a demo with the number fully worked out so that we can work on our side of it before we go into the studio — that was how he wrote 'My Generation'.

Pete Townshend, on singing 'My Generation' fifteen years later: Well, now, of course, it feels totally ridiculous. Maybe we should change the words. We do now slow it down to a Jimmy Reed

R&B tempo . . . which is more suitable for me tired old legs.

'I'm A Boy'

Pete Townshend: The chord structure in 'I'm A Boy' and the opening chords in 'Pinball Wizard' were directly influenced by that piece of music by Purcell, which I'm sure a lot of our fans will flinch at.

'Happy Jack'

Pete Townshend: My father used to play saxophone in a band for the season on the Isle Of Man when I was a kid. There was no character called Happy Jack, but I played on the beach a lot and it's just my memories of some of the weirdos who lived on the sand.

'Pictures Of Lily'

Pete Townshend: It's all about a boy who can't sleep at night so his dad gives him some dirty pictures to look at. Then he falls in love with the girl in the pictures which is too bad because she is dead.

John Entwistle: It's all about wanking . . . Townshend going through his sexual traumas, something that he did quite often. I sometimes think you could say that record represents our smutty period, or to be more refined, our Blue Period!

Pete Townshend: John and I used to exchange pictures like that when we were at school. We used to go into grubby little shops to buy them . . . looking at dirty pictures is a normal part of adolescence.

Pete Townshend: A lot of demos have been so good, in fact, that it's scared us out of making recordings . . . 'Magic Bus' — we didn't want to do it. I listened to the demo and I thought the demo was good but that we're never gonna catch it on record. It's gonna bring us all down. Let's forget it, let's do something else; and Kit was going, "No, we're going to do it, we're going to do it, we're going to do it, you're going to learn every line, every little detail, every precious thing in the demonstration record you're gonna catch and you're gonna copy it if necessary." What happened is, in the end we gave up and we thought, "Oh, we'll do it," and we went down and we did it completely differently, but it all came together and we went up and thanked him for making us do it.

John Entwistle's songs.

John Entwistle: There's too many people composing love songs, religious songs and serious things like that. If it's my bag to write 'orrible sick songs which disturb people some way, then I'm content that's my job.

John Entwistle: I find something very repellent in the usual love song. The first thing I think of

when you mention love is somebody leaving somebody else. My wife often asks me about that. I just can't do it. I can write about spiders and alcoholics and suicides, but when it comes to love, I'm stuck. The only love song I'd consider writing is a love song about a dog, because that would mean more to a lot of people than a love song about humans. You don't really know if a dog loves you. If you didn't feed it, it'd probably eat you.

'Tommy'

Pete Townshend: It was Kit who conceived the idea of an extended pop work. He suggested that we write an opera to fill in a ten-minute gap in an album called 'While He's Away' (later retitled 'A Quick One'). No-one writes a ten-minute song. How can you sustain their interest? Which seems ridiculous now. I linked up about six pieces of music and it was very successful.

Pete Townshend: I had such grand aims and yet such a deep respect for rock tradition and particularly Who tradition, which was then firmly embedded in singles. But I always wanted to do bigger, grander things, and I felt that rock should too, and I always felt sick that rock was looked upon as a kind of second best to other art forms, that there was some dispute as to whether rock was art. Rock is art and a million other things as well — it's an indescribable form of communication and entertainment combined, and it's a two-way thing with very complex but real feedback processes as well. I don't think there's anything to match it. So I felt at the time that the only way to get into a position where the whole incredible thing was portrayed truly, or what it was to have something that appeared on the surface to be very grand but which when you got to the root of it you found was all rock and roll singles strung together.

Pete Townshend: I felt very much at the time of writing 'Tommy' that I had to move away from the druggies that surround the group, the people that really saw The Who as a heavy psychedelic band, the people who'd put tabs of acid in your coffee before you went on stage . . . I felt devastated by that.

Pete Townshend: It wasn't the obsession with my own physical ugliness that is the root-key to 'Tommy', although that's what motivated me to be a pop star. I was teased at school about having a big nose and I was never very tall. I felt great vengeance at all the kinds of teasing, especially the most subtle kinds. I had quite a lot of hate, but I don't think any of that manifests itself in 'Tommy'.

Pete Townshend: As a gag, when we were working on it, we started to call it a rock opera, knowing full well it wasn't a true opera at all. I didn't need the music critics to tell me it wasn't an opera — I've probably listened to as much straight opera as many of them have. But the tag stuck and we realised it was maybe a bit fanciful, but in spite of that we quite liked the idea.

Roger Daltrey: Rock opera? It was a rock hype at first. We called it an opera for something to do. But the kids took it seriously. They came to see us perform it and we got feedback from that and it became something . . . alive. *Very* strange.

John Entwistle: All I know is that when we were recording the damn thing, nobody knew what it was all about or how it would end. It was only when it was decided to make 'Tommy' into a double album instead of a single that it became much easier to work out the story line.

Roger Daltrey: 'Tommy' was the next stepping stone from 'My Generation'.

Pete Townshend: I think that despite the fact that the album is my own little thing and the motivation is not completely understood by the rest of the group even, it's still the first group effort really, since so much of the other stuff we did was gimmick-laden advertising schmatter. This is working toward a more unified project.

Pete Townshend: I mean, what other three musicians would have put up with all my bullshit in order to get this album out? It's my apple, right? It's my whole trip, coming from Baba (Meher Baba, *Townshend's Indian avatar*). And they just sat there, let it come out, and then leapt upon it and gave it an extra boot. It's an incredible group to write for, because you know it's going to work out right. And I've written other songs, which I won't mention. I've only ever had hits with The Who. And hit records are very near and dear to me.

Pete Townshend: What I think is good about 'Tommy' is not that it's a rock opera or that it's the first or the last — that's if you assume that there's gonna be any more. What I feel is very important about 'Tommy' is that as a band it was our first conscious departure out of the adolescent area. It was something that wasn't the same old pilled-up adolescent brand of music. We'd finished with that and we didn't know which way to go. That's why we went through that very funny period of 'Happy Jack' and 'Dogs'.

It was also a terrifying period for me as The Who's only ideas man. For instance, though 'I Can See For Miles' was released after 'Happy Jack', I'd written it in 1966 but we had kept it in the can for ages because it was going to be The Who's ace-in-the-hole. The truth is, I really got lost after 'Happy Jack' and then when 'I Can See For Miles' bombed-out in Britain, I thought, "What the hell can I do now?" The pressures

DEAF, DUMB AND BLIND TOMMY STANDS INSIDE ACID QUEEN'S 'IRON MAIDEN'

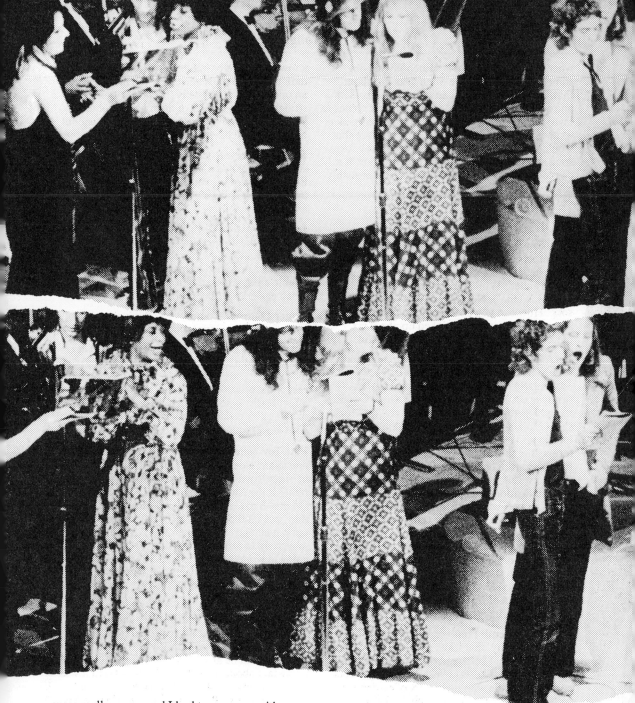

'TOMMY' LIVE AT RAINBOW, 1972

were really on me and I had to come up with something very quick and that's how Tommy emerged from a few rough ideas I'd been messing about with.

Roger Daltrey: I don't think 'Tommy' is The Who's best piece of work.

Roger Daltrey: I don't think 'Tommy' held the band back — it's just that nobody wanted to listen to what else we were doing. 'Who's Next' holds up much better, but nobody wanted to take it seriously because it was just nine songs and no great thing about a bloody spastic.

Pete Townshend: It's definitely not a total success. I've had a lot of kids come up to me and say, "Well, look man, you've spent two years on it, why didn't you spend three years on it and tighten up some of the bad things about it?"

Pete Townshend: I think the greatest thing that I've seen lately about 'Tommy' is the Radio Times' feature and there were three interviews; one with Nik Cohn who says he thinks 'Tommy' was sparked off by his book in which there was a deaf and blind pinball champion; Mike McKinley

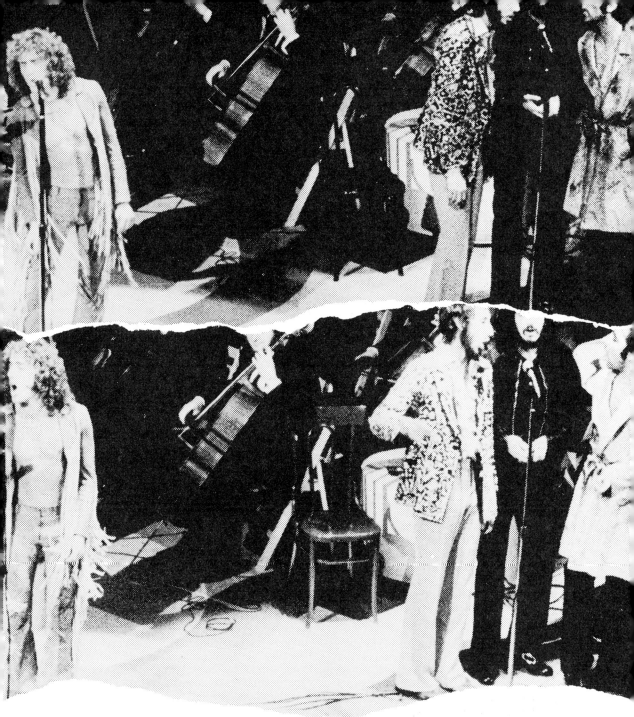

said he thought 'Tommy' came because I was interested in this spiritual master Meher Baba; and Roger said it was Kit Lambert's idea. The point is that I don't really know. All I know is that I was talking about opera for a long time before 'Tommy' came about and I just don't really know how it emerged. It was such a long, evolved process. A lot came together in the last few weeks of writing. I had ideas to write a rock opera or an opera opera. At one time I was studying orchestrations and listening to Wagner and all kinds of amazing things trying to get into full scale grand opera and I was going to enlist

Arthur Brown whose voice I thought somewhere between a Wagnerian tenor and Screaming Jay Hawkins and have him as the lead singer. The idea that I worked on before 'Tommy' was called 'Rael' and that was condensed into a four minute single.It turned out to be a track on 'The Who Sell Out' album and immediately after that I started to think I should really get to grips — it was a personal thing I think. I was thinking that it might even be done outside The Who. In other words, I'd write a few singles and things to keep the band happy, but in the meantime I'd be working on this rather grand thing on the side. And in the end it all sort of came together. I don't think it would have happened had it not been for the band's added energy, and also Kit Lambert's involvement was very important.

John Entwistle: By the time it was released, I for one was sick to death of 'Tommy'. I have only ever played the record at home about twenty times and never all the way through. On stage now, we do a selection, and that's it.

Pete Townshend: To sum 'Tommy' up is impossible. It sounds so fucking ridiculous, and the story *is* ridiculous.

Pete Townshend: What I was dead keen to do was to make the thing multi-layered, so that it had a story, that there were the musical aspects of it, so that the social aspects were well defined — rock and roll, exploitation, organised religion, drugs, exploitation of drugs, children's cruelty to children, sex . . . all those things. I wanted those things to be there to make the thing real and — what's the word? — aware, I suppose. And the other thing I wanted to do was to make the thing have a spiritual meaning, to make the point that individual experience is what counts, and that 'Tommy's' experiences had earned him a kind of super-consciousness which everybody else was on the way to having anyway, but because they see and are attracted to this miraculously charismatic figure, they're sidetracked into believing that this is the way to do it. They lose the sense that their own lives are tailor-made for them. That they must change is the lesson. And in the end the thing that I really wanted to get across — and it's very ill defined as to what 'Tommy' actually is and I haven't really adopted a stance on it — but he's definitely not a Meher Baba. He's a . . . a saint? Maybe just ordinary, ordinary and invigorated by being ordinary after so many years of not being so.

Pete Townshend: I was very mystified by the fact that 'Tommy' was so financially successful because it was the first really good, well-intended thing that I'd ever done — the first time that I'd really wanted to do something good. And in that way I suppose I was trying to put out spiritual ideas, and it then embarrassed me that it had to make money. This is it, put on your Salvation Army uniform and your Rolls Royce arrives in the post, your place in heaven is guaranteed right here on earth.

Pete Townshend: I didn't write 'Tommy' in any kind of chronological order. I already had some of the material — the Doctor song, 'Pinball Wizard' and the finale. The first rundown of the idea I put on a graph! It was intended to show 'Tommy' from the outside and his impressions going on inside him.

'Pinball Wizard'

Pete Townshend: It's about life's games, playing the machine — the boy and his machine, the disciples with theirs, the scores, results, colours, vibrations and actions. I don't happen to be divine at the moment. I can't express the magnificence of divinity in music, but I can express the grooviness of being a pinball champ because I'm a pop star which is very close. The absurdity of being a pinball champion!

'The Acid Queen'

Pete Townshend: The song's not about just acid; it's the whole drug thing, the drink thing, the sex thing wrapped into one big ball. It's about how you get it laid on you that you haven't lived if you haven't fucked forty birds, taken sixty trips, drunk fourteen pints or whatever. Society — people — force you. She represents this force. On a number of occasions I've got this sinister, feline, sexual thing about acid, that it's inherently female. I don't know if I'm right . . . it's fickle enough.

'Live At Leeds'

Pete Townshend: I've been planning a live album for ages. And we recorded all the shows on the last American tour thinking that would be where we would get the best material. When we got back we had eighty hours of tape and, well, we couldn't sort that lot out, so we booked the Pye mobile studio and took it to Leeds. It turned out to be one of the best and most enjoyable gigs we've ever done.

'Who's Next'

John Entwistle: This was our next major concept. Originally it was going to be called 'Lifehouse' and incorporate film footage. Basically, the project centred around The Who living with its audience. We did a couple of experimental things down at The Young Vic and then the whole thing fell through. When we started, 'Lifehouse' was to be a double album. Half of it ended up on this album, and another four tracks are on 'Odds And Sods'.

'Baba O'Riley'

Pete Townshend: This was a number I wrote while I was doing these experiments with tapes on the synthesizer. Among my plans for the concert at The Young Vic was to take a person out of the audience and feed information — height, weight, astrological details, beliefs and behaviour etc — about that person into the synthesizer. The synthesizer would then select notes from the

TINA TURNER AS THE ACID QUEEN IN 'TOMMY'

pattern of that person. It would be like translating a person into music. On this particular track I programmed details about the life of Meher Baba and that provides the backing for the number.

'Won't Get Fooled Again'

Pete Townshend: It's really a bit of a weird song. The first verse sounds like a revolution song and the second like somebody getting tired of it. Basically, it's the same vein as 'We're Not Gonna Take It' (from 'Tommy'). It's an angry anti-establishment song. It's anti people who are negative. A song against the revolution because the revolution is only a revolution and a revolution is not going to change anything at all in the long run, and a lot of people are going to get hurt. When I wrote 'We're Not Gonna Take It' it was really we're not gonna take fascism. 'Won't Get Fooled Again' I wrote at a time when I was getting barraged by people at the Eel Pie Island commune. They live opposite me. There was like

a love affair going on between me and them. They dug me because I was like a figurehead . . . in a group . . . and I dug them because I could see what was going on over there. At one point there was an amazing scene where the commune was really working, but then the acid started flowing and I got on the end of some psychotic conversations. And I just thought "Oh fuck it!". I call it The Glastonbury Syndrome.

'Quadrophenia'

Pete Townshend: Roger and I have different ideas about 'Quadrophenia'. I think the story line isn't so complicated, it bears much explaining. A kid sits on a rock and remembers the things that have happened in the last few days. I think if you explain the story line too much it demeans all the other things in the music, makes it too Tanglewood Tales. The story, after all, is just a peg to hang ideas on. When Roger gets too literal about the story I have to cut it and make it lighter.

Roger Daltrey: The thing we did with 'Quadrophenia', we bullshitted it up so much

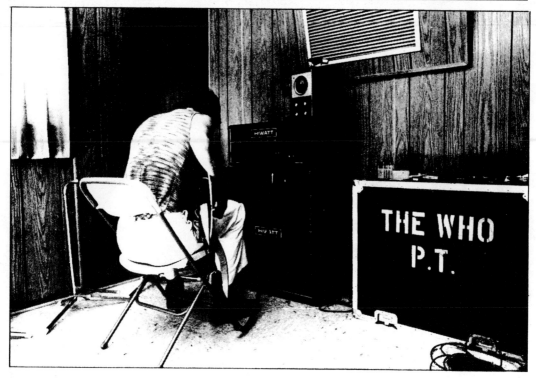

there was nothing left for the kids to think about, you know. It was done for them.

'Who By Numbers'

Roger Daltrey: There was a breakthrough on the side of the musical content because we had a serious discussion about how The 'Oo had worked itself into a niche, hence there's a lot of different feels on the album. That's cool. I know it's only my personal opinion, but if Pete would explain things like 'They're All In Love' then I think it would help for a better understanding. Truthfully that's one song that I really didn't wanna sing until Pete clarified certain aspects. I knew what the first two verses were about but the last one had me completely baffled. 'Goodbye All You Punks' is a goodbye to all your nostalgic bastards who are still living on the nostalgic part of The 'Oo because nostalgia just ain't no good to us. We're not past it, we're just different.

Pete Townshend: 'Who By Numbers' was revealing, I suppose, because it was all I had left at the time. I just thought, "What am I gonna do, because I'm fucked up, not writing anything?" There was one little chink in the armour, and that's the ukelele track ('Blue, Red And Grey').

'They're All In Love'

Goodbye all you punks stay young and stay high/Hand me my chequebook and I'll crawl off to die

Pete Townshend: What the lines are about is that we went in to sue Kit Lambert. It's not really what it seems to be about. Punks didn't mean what it does today. Punks is what I used to call the New York fans who used to try and get you by the ears and pin you down and take you home in a cardboard box. The song was about what the band had become. It was about money, about law courts, about lawyers and accountants. Those things had *never* mattered and the band had a backlog of tax problems and unpaid royalties. We had to deal with it. I really felt like crawling off and dying.

John Entwistle, on the 'Who By Numbers' cover: The cover drawing only took me an hour, but the dots took about three hours. I took it down to the studio while we were mixing and got the worst artist in the room to fill it in. Discovered I'd left two inside legs out.

'Squeeze Box'

Pete Townshend: I wrote this song called 'Squeeze Box'. I went out and bought an accordion and learned to play it in about ten minutes, so it's a devastatingly simple song.

'Imagine A Man'

Pete Townshend: It just might be a key to the way that rock could grow old. It's about that feeling of being . . . not a failure, but over the hill. It's about that pathetic, pointless, tragic situation

80

that a man gets into where — well, I've never
been a great puller of birds so it's not auto-
biographical, but for example where he can't pull
without a big scene, and he's not really all that
mad on drinking any more, and to tell the truth he
really does quite like watching television. It's a
bit of an effort to get out on the pitch and play
football on Saturdays, and to be perfectly honest
he does quite like sex on a regular basis so he can
build himself up to it and not let the old lady

down. It's that type of thing, and it's about how
incredible all that is. And I realised after I'd
written it what an amazingly perceptive piece of
writing it was, and that either I was getting like
that or somebody that I knew intimately was
getting that way. Then of course I realised the
song was about me. And if The Who end up

recording this song, then it will definitely be a landmark in our career because it's got the kind of honesty there is in a song like 'Substitute'.

'Who Are You'

Pete Townshend: I'm really quite relieved that we managed to get the new album done. But I'm pleased with the writing. I particularly like 'Trick Of The Light', a song John wrote. And I'm glad I managed to get 'Guitar And Pen' and 'Music Must Change' to be as optimistic *and* razor-edged. They're not screaming vitriol, but they're still quite hard . . . not in the aggressive way that 'Who Are You' is hard. That's probably the most archetypal, old-fashioned Who-sounding track on the album . . . very much in the tradition of 'Won't Get Fooled Again'.

Life At The Top.

Moon madness.

Keith Moon: A lot of things I do are done to show how people react to certain situations. I love the unexpected, and I love to make people laugh. To me that's what life's all about. You can't really plan anything, and I suppose that's one of the reasons why I don't often hurt myself. I never ever consider I might actually sustain an injury. If I did, then I'd probably get hurt. Now if I had some kind of morbid death wish, I never would have survived any of those times when I've crashed my cars. I suppose it's luck, and the fact that I never think anything could happen to me.

Keith Moon, on his twenty-first Birthday Party: That's how I lost my front tooth. In Flint, Michigan. We had a show that night. We were all around the Holiday Inn pool, Herman's Hermits and myself. I was twenty-one and they started giving me presents. Somebody gave me a portable bar and somebody else the portable booze. I'd started drinking about ten o'clock in the morning and I can't remember the show. Then the record company had booked a big room in the hotel, one of the conference rooms, for a party. As the hours went on it got louder and louder, and everybody started getting well out of their minds, well stoned. The pool was the obvious target. Everybody started jumping in the pool with their clothes on. The Premier Drum Company had given us a huge birthday cake with like five drums stacked up on top of each other. As the party degenerated into a slanging, I picked up the cake, all five tiers, and hurled it in the throng. People'd started picking up the pieces and hurling it about. Everybody was covered in marzipan and icing sugar and fruit-cake. The manager heard the fracas and came in. There it was, his great carpet, stained irrevocably with marzipan and fruitcake trodden in, and everybody dancing about with their trousers off. By the time the sheriff came in I was standing there in my underpants. I ran out, jumped into the first car I came to, which was a brand new Lincoln Continental. It was parked on a slight hill and when I took the handbrake off, it started to roll and it smashed straight through the pool surround and the whole Lincoln Continental went into the Holiday Inn swimming pool with me in it.

So there I was, sitting in the eight-foot-six in the driver's seat of a Lincoln Continental, underwater. And the water was pouring in — coming in through the bloody pedal holes in the floorboard, you know, squirting in through the windows. In a startling moment of logic I said, "Well, I can't open the doors until the pressure is the same . . ." It's amazing how I remembered those things from my physics class! I knew I'd have to wait until the pressure was the same.

So I'm sitting there, thinking about my situation, as the water creeps up me nose. Today I can think of less outrageous ways of going than drowning in a Lincoln Continental in a Holiday Inn swimming pool, but at the time I had no thoughts of death whatsoever. There was none of that all-my-life-passing-before-my-eyes-in-a-flash. I was busy planning. I knew if I panicked, I'd have had it. So when there's just enough air in the top of the car to take a gulp I fill up me lungs, throw open the door and go rising to the top of the pool. I figured there'll be quite a crowd gathered by now. After all, I'd been down there underwater for some time. I figured they'd be so grateful I was alive, they'd overlook the Lincoln Continental. But no. There's only one person standing there and he's the pool cleaner and he's got to have the pool clean in the morning and he's furious.

So I went back to the party, streaming water, still in me underpants. The first person I see is the sheriff and he's got his hand on his gun. Sod this! And I ran, I started to leg it out the door, and I slipped on a piece of marzipan and fell flat on my face and knocked out my teeth.

I spent the remainder of the night under the custody of the sheriff at a dentist's. The dentist couldn't give me any anaesthetic because I was pissed out of my mind. So he had to rip out what was left of the tooth and put a false one in, and the next day I spent a couple of hours in the nick. The boys had chartered me a plane because they had to leave on an earlier flight. The sheriff took me out in the law car and he puts me on the plane and says, "Son, don't ever dock in Flint, Michigan again." I said, "Dear boy, I wouldn't

destroyed a piano, completely destroyed it. Reduced it to a kindling. And don't forget the carpet. And the Lincoln Continental in the bottom of the pool. So I got a bill for $24,000. I wasn't earning half that on the tour, and I'd spent everything by the time I got to Flint, Michigan. I was in debt past my eyebrows before this happened. Luckily Herman's Hermits and the boys split it up, about thirty of us all gave a thousand dollars each. It was like a religious ceremony as we all came up and dropped a thousand dollars into a big hat and sent it off to the Holiday Inn with a small compliments card with "Balls" written across it — and the words "See you soon."

dream of it." And I was lisping around the new tooth.

By now I'd learned how destructive we'd all been. During the merriment someone had upset all the fire extinguishers and turned them on all the cars in the car park. Six of them had to have new paint jobs; the paint peeled off. We'd also

John Entwistle: He never drove a car into the swimming pool. He couldn't even drive. He hit the sheriff with the cake, because the person he threw it at ducked and he started running, except he was so pissed he tripped and fell over and smashed his teeth. So the sheriff drove him to the dentist's and we all waited while they operated on him without any anaesthetic . . . 'cause he was drunk. He was whimpering for about two days. He didn't even *see* a swimming pool that night!

Keith Moon: I suppose to most people I'm probably seen as an amiable idiot . . . a genial twit.

Keith Moon: I suppose when I stop to analyse my lack of closeness to other people I'd conclude I was basically lonely and unable to communicate other than at a superficial level. But I'm

happy the way I am, living in a whirl of incident and excitement.

Keith Moon: My way of life is not conducive to any kind of stable family relationship. I am not close to my daughter Mandy. I think she's nine, but I forget.

Keith Moon: I need everything that is going to be offered me — the birds, the booze and to smash things up, perhaps. The one thing which scares me is drugs. I do not need the kind of illusions which drugs bring. The public aspect of my life is an illusion anyway . . . an hallucination. I don't need an hallucination within an hallucination.

Keith Moon: For years I have been a drinker. Alcohol gives life a pleasant blur. But earlier this year (1972) drink was taking over too much; I was up to two bottles of brandy and a bottle of champagne a day. So I went on a cure. Now I drink in a controlled way. I never drink before going on stage.

Keith Moon: If I had not been a pop star I would have been a wild-living spendthrift scientist. Probably I'd have ended up in prison. At school I loved physics and chemistry and did very well at them.

Keith Moon: I even met my wife, Kim, when I was seventeen, when she came to a dance in Bournemouth with a girlfriend who was a groupie. Within a year Kim and I were married. But that made no difference to my interest in the rest of the talent around. Marriage didn't calm me down. I never was a faithful husband. For a few years Kim managed to turn a blind eye to my raving, but she got more and more fed up with the whole thing. Before our divorce I had a succession of girlfriends, some of whose names I don't even remember.

Keith Moon: All the band ever says to me when they're in the studio singing is "Get out". Then I act as barman 'cause they all get terrible dry throats and I have to keep on pouring out the brandy all the time. Also, if I'm in the studio, looning about while they're trying to lay down a vocal track, they can't sing if they're laughing at me dressed up as a wasp. You know, there's nothing worse when you're trying to be serious than to have a human wasp flying all over the studio.

Kenny Jones: The only time I got into the car with Keith coming from the gig, we're going through the middle of Glasgow and he's got these inflatable plastic legs, a loudspeaker and a microphone. He's screaming "Rape, rape!" and waving these legs through the car window. We caused so much havoc that as we drove out of town about a hundred squad cars came out of nowhere. They

KEITH MOON WITH RINGO STARR IN FILM 'COUNTDOWN'

KEITH MOON WITH WIFE KIM AND DAUGHTER MANDY

thought we were raping someone, and it was all hands up against the wall. Back at the hotel, we explained to the police we were just messing about.

Keith Moon, on filming 'Countdown' with Harry Nilsson: We were supposed to be on the set at six, but it was nine before everybody was there. Then someone brought out a bottle of brandy. Me, I think. And Peter Frampton said, "No, no, too early" and some of the others said no. But Harry was standing there with a half pint mug. I knew at that moment it was destiny that put us together. So we were drinking brandy at nine, and, thanks to Mal Evans, white wine all the rest of the day. Then around six o'clock somebody came around and slipped little envelopes into our hands. It was a pay packet. I hadn't had a pay packet in ten years. And Harry'd never had one. We were pretty well out of it and we looked at each other and then tore up one hundred and seventy pounds in one pound notes, threw it up in the air and danced about, cackling like little school boys. Dancing and leaping about, clutching bottles of Blue Nun Liebfraumilch in our hands, singing, "We're millionaires, aren't we?".

Keith Moon: There are things that have happened to me that have made me wonder where I went wrong . . . things of a personal nature, like my relationship with my wife. They're the things that make you think most . . . because one is far more deeply involved. Like when I was looning off to Copenhagen a couple of years ago, and Kim left me for a time. It was then I realised I'd taken the wrong turning, and so I backtracked and learned from my mistakes. You see, I love Kim very much and the group, and therefore I wouldn't do anything to hurt them anyway.

Keith Moon: I get bored, you see. There was a time in Saskatoon, in Canada. It was another Holiday Inn and I was bored. Now, when I get bored, I rebel. I said, "Fuck it, fuck the lot of you." And I took out me hatchet and chopped the hotel room to bits. The television. The chairs. The dresser. The cupboard doors. The bed. The lot of it. It happens all the time.

Keith Moon: I have spent around £250,000 in payments for damaging hotels and friends' homes. When I've done damage at a friend's house I come back sheepishly next day and offer to "put things right", which means I'm willing to foot the bill.

Keith Moon: At heart I cannot accept that I am a well-known rock and roll star, and one of the greatest drummers in the world. I can't believe

that person on the television is really me. The Keith Moon the public knows is a myth, even if I have created him. The real me is the person who sits at home having a cup of tea with his old lady, Annettee (Annettee Walter-Lax, the Swedish model who was Moon's long-standing girlfriend). The hotel smashing is one way I get relief from the public image. I have no temper. I do it in a spirit of amusement rather than anger.

Keith Moon, on his divorce at the end of September 1973: The pressures on us have been tremendous because of the nature of my work. I have been away from home for long periods. And my wife has been subjected to all kinds of verbal and physical abuse — even having eggs thrown at her. I suppose that despite the luxury my wife lives in, me and the fans have not made her life very easy. She just couldn't handle fame. It got so bad she resented pop . . . even hated it. She

didn't want to come to shows, didn't want to talk about music. She even tried to get me to change because she didn't like people laughing at me. But if you're a clown, you've got to put up with that, haven't you? She was always on at me to grow up. Well, I do crazy things sometimes like driving the Rolls at eighty mph around the garden. That's the sort of person I am. I thought she had adjusted to it. It seems she hadn't . . . when I was out at night working she never really believed me. She thought I was having a high old time. But then some of it was my fault I suppose. I mean it's bloody hard to come off stage after all the elation of the music and the screaming fans, and then drive home and talk about domestic matters like whether the kid's front teeth are growing crooked or straight. Kim used to get particularly upset when she thought I was being juvenile. You know, everyone thought it was a

KEITH MOON WITH GIRLFRIEND ANNETTEE WALTER-LAX

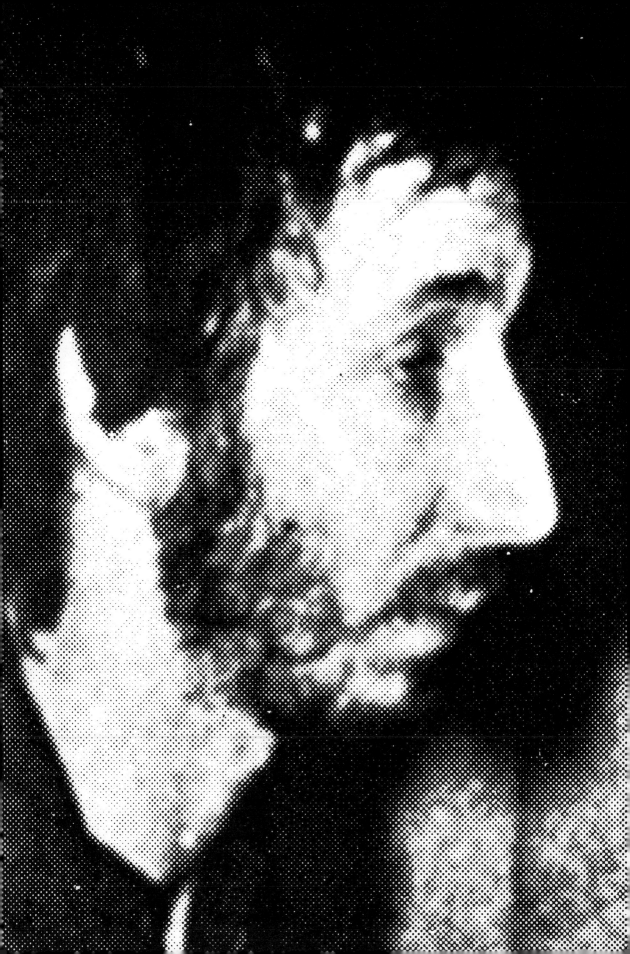

hoot when I drove the £65,000 Lincoln Continental into the swimming pool of an hotel in America on my twenty-first birthday. But Kim was not amused. Oh no.

Pete Townshend: To me Keith Moon was born a star, is a star and will always be a star — even when he's begging for pennies down on the river bank. He'll still be a bigger star than Bryan Ferry, Mott the Hoople and David Bowie all rolled into one.

Drugs.

Keith Moon: I think we just sort of grew out of drugs. The drugs aren't necessary now. They were then, as a crutch. We went through just about everything. Not Roger so much. He smoked, but that was it. The rest of us went through the same stages everybody goes through — the bloody drug corridor. You know. We were no exception. Eventually we stopped rucking about with the chemicals and started on the grape. Drinking suited the group a lot better. When we started drinking, that's when it all started getting together. We're all pretty good drinkers. After the show there's always the celebration drink, or the non-celebration drink. Then there's always the clubs — John and I, generally, go clubbing. We just like the social side of drinking. Everybody I know is a drinker. I've met some of my best friends in pubs.

Pete Townshend: I feel that there's a spiritual process going on in every person's head that's so overwhelmingly complex and so beautifully balanced, and acid just feeds on the distortion of that balance. People find pleasure in distorting the balance. But the human being is such a beautifully equipped piece of machinery that it's very spiritually disturbing to topple it, and think that it's good. If you know you're throwing yourself out of balance, like when you're drunk, you hate yourself, so that's all right. But when you trip, for some reason you love yourself. You don't realise you were better equipped as you were. Each trip is just a side street, and before you know it, you're back where you were. Each trip is more disturbing than the one that follows, till eventually the side street becomes a dead end. Not only spiritually, which is the most important, but mentally it can stop you thinking. Physically it can fuck you up. People are falling out of trees and all this bullshit. Acid has happened and there was obviously a purpose for it — the acceleration of spiritual thinking — otherwise I believe it wouldn't have happened. So I'm against what it has done. Actually, I did enjoy my trips but the acid song ('The Acid Queen') is supposed to show the potential of acid as a spiritual push and knock it down as a danger of reducing the power of man in society.

MIKE McINNERNEY

Pete Townshend: I used to frequent the UFO Club which is where I met Mike McInnerney and Karen and all that lot, everybody. We used to get that Swiss stuff (acid), which was real Sandoz stuff, which is really incredibly pure, and then we went to the Monterey pop festival and I took Karen with me — we weren't married then, and the famous Owsley showed up. He's The Grateful Dead's sort of road manager and drug producer. He was on the research team that invented LSD and knew how to make it and used to make his own brand called STP which was much more powerful. And we took some on the plane coming home . . . and it was bloody terrible. I mean, you wouldn't believe it. I mean I had to . . . You know when they say under Japanese torture occasionally sometimes if it's horrific enough the person actually gets the feeling that they're leaving their body. In this case I had to do just that, abandon my body, there's no doubt about it, that's exactly what happened. I said, "Fuck this, I can't stand any more." And I was free of the trip. This is really the truth, right. And I was just floating in mid-air looking at myself in a chair, for about an hour and a half. And then I would rest and I would go back in again and it would be the same. And I was just like zap, completely unconscious as far as the outside world was concerned, but I was very much alive, in that, you know, like alive, crawling alive. Anyway, the thing about STP as distinct from LSD is the hump, the nasty bit. It goes on for about sixteen hours rather than ten. And just to walk or just to do anything fundamentally organic is very very tricky. But eventually it tailed off and then you get like instead of a night's

lovely planning it, nice colourful images, you get about a week of it and you get a week of trying to repiece your ego, remember who you were and what you are and stuff like that. So that made me stop taking psychedelics.

Roger Daltrey: I've done almost everything — except the hard ones. Seem to do a lot of pot which I think calmed me down a lot. But the last time I had a joint I didn't even get high, and I used to do a hell of a lot once. Used to do an ounce of hash every night. I used to love it. I used to get blotto.

Pete Townshend: I don't use dope, for instance, but I'm often with people who do. Baba changed my life in that respect. I don't normally get involved with the usual group road scenes, dirty parties, or any of the kind of thing you see on Faces posters, but it goes on around me. I mean, Baba lovers in the States are incredulous. They

98

walk into my room and go "Jah Baba", which means "victory to Baba", and there's a room full of people . . . broken guitars on the floor, piles of whisky bottles, television sets out in the street, lemon curd on the wall. They just can't equate the two things. I'm not saying I'm sitting there aloof, like the bloody lighthouse in the middle of the stormy sea — I'm affected, I'm involved, and part of the time I'm doing it — it's just that Baba is strong enough to keep hold of you, and it's possible for you to keep hold of him whatever you're doing.

Sex.

Roger Daltrey: I was the original pop star, knocking off as many birds as you could get in the one night . . . and loved them all. I got married when I was still playing at the pub — at an early age — when I was about twenty. She was a great girl. But that was a mistake. It was

ENTWISTLE WITH WIFE ALISON

either the marriage or the group. I chose the group. To get the group off the ground it was a one hundred per cent twenty-four hour day — and marriage just didn't fit in anywhere. I mean birds were just good for your ego. Rock and roll was good for their ego. Girls just made themselves so incredibly available. They'd do anything. They're fucking an image. Not just a person. I don't know what their image of me is. I'm a pig. That's what it is. The old style groupies don't exist anymore. Originally they were great.

They used to make life bearable on the road. The old American groupie scene doesn't exist any more either. The last few tours there were new style groupies — obviously in it to be seen with the rock and roll bands. That *seems* to be more important than anything else.

Roger Daltrey: There's something about a Y-bone steak I can't resist. Fortunately I've got a missus that isn't particularly bothered by it. She's one in a million, my missus.

Pete Townshend: The whole process of sex is embodied in just the rock and roll rhythm — like gospel music or like native chants or something. Just banging the table is like it's the demand and it's also the satiation as well. You bang on the table and in the same process you masturbate, you know. At the end of the show you're finished, you know, you've had it. You've come your lot and the show's over.

Pete Townshend: The relationships that had a sexual culmination have been sort of empty, lousy things and I tended to push them into the background. The ones I treasured were usually platonic. I'm not a great believer in promiscuity. I can remember when I was at school the general idea was that men were after sex and women were after relationships. I think it's half-way between the two. I always look for something which is more than just sex.

DALTREY WITH WIFE HEATHER

Politics.

Keith Moon: Abbie Hoffman jumped on the stage at Woodstock and started protesting and the kids didn't cheer until Pete whacked him with his guitar. If he wants to preach, let him do it on a soap box, not on our stage.

Roger Daltrey: I think you should pay the people on welfare enough to live. What is such a shame is that people go to work and can't really earn much more because it's all taken away in tax . . . and the tax is all wasted on more government to dish out less welfare. Just suppose I invest money, whatever that money makes as investment income I'm paying about ninety-eight per cent tax on it. And yet that's the only way England's going to become great, by people investing in England. If you really love England shove your fucking money into it. But why put your money in it if you don't get anything? I mean inflation is twenty-five per cent. I live in England because I like English people. I really love England. Money isn't everything to me. I'm not poor. Fortunately up to two years ago there were schemes where you could earn money abroad and not pay tax on it . . . which has all gone to pot now. We did earn some money through those schemes, which were perfectly legal. I'd hate to think what any new group's going to do. Well, most of the groups have left already, haven't they? Anyone who starts to make it leaves — I suppose financially they've got to. I don't mind paying that amount of tax — it's what they do with it I don't like. If I thought it would go to old age pensioners to increase their pension, but it doesn't. Every time they put up taxes it's always just another department for this or another for that. Look at the amount of civil servants . . . I'd certainly lower taxes, definitely I think it is the main problem in this country — overtaxed and overgoverned.

Roger Daltrey: Modern society doesn't leave much bloody room for your own identity, does it? That's why rock and roll's been so successful.

Roger Daltrey: Nye Bevan was a real socialist. He wasn't just a fucking member of the Labour Party. He cared about people. Which is a lot of difference — the fucking Labour Party doesn't. It cares about the fucking Labour Party. This is why they're not bloody socialists at all.

John Entwistle: It's really difficult for someone in our position to live in England. The income tax is stupid. It makes you feel like going down to get your dole money, trying to get some of it back. The country has never given me anything at all. I've never had anything out of it. What's the use of National Health if you have to wait six months?

Money.

Keith Moon: We were smashing up probably ten times if not more than we were earning. We've been going successfully for ten years, but we've only made money in the last three. It took us five years to pay off three years, our most destructive period.

Keith Moon: Some time ago my accountant told me I had a lot of money. I said "How much? I mean am I a millionaire?" "Well, technically yes." So I said, "What should I do about it". And he said, "Well, obviously if you've got that much money and you've got these tax bills, it's logical to spend money so that you can claim money against tax that's owed." "I see . . . so I should spend money?" "Well, yes you should." So six weeks later I'd spent it all. I'd bought four houses, a hotel, eight cars, a swimming pool, tennis courts, expensive wrist watches — that fell apart — a riverside bungalow, furnished in French Renaissance period furniture. I'd spent it all. It was gone. Ha Ha Ha Ha . . .

Keith Moon: We're more involved with giving a fucking good show than we are with money. If it costs us every fucking penny we're making, it doesn't worry us. I'd rather give a good show than make money.

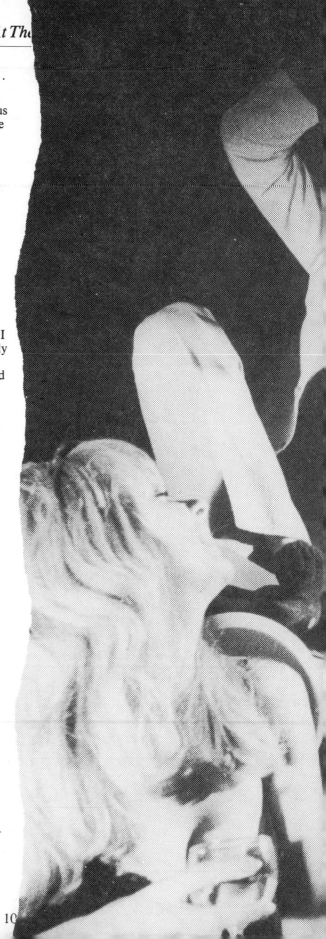

Keith Moon: They're always saying I'm a Capitalist pig. I suppose I am, but, ah . . . it ah . . it's good for my drumming, I think.

Pete Townshend: I know Roger's very conscious all the time of the money set-up. I think it's quite simply because he can't sleep at night unless he does actually know what we're earning. But that's probably because he's probably never spent the way Keith and I have — which is why we don't care how much we've got. We spend what we need to spend, and then we ask questions later. I've never got into the red, because of my writing money, which has kept me a wee bit ahead of the group, but Keith has occasionally gone into the red through over-spending. But in the end you just say, "We're just going to have to do a few more tours or something."

Roger Daltrey: It's not that I'm money-mad or anything. It's just that nobody else gives a fuck. I don't want to worry about the money and it really haunts me that I have to. But somebody has to look after it. I've seen so many groups get fucked over by mis-management and I refuse to let it happen to The Who.

Roger Daltrey: I'd rather be down here living in the country earning £14 a week than chasing a big wage in London.

Keith Moon: I came out of the end of our last English tour with a net profit of £46.70.

Stardom.

Roger Daltrey: I wish I could become Charlie Bloggs. I'm pissed off with it because I feel it's not me. I'm not a living legend. A load of old bollocks. I don't really want to be A Pop Star, believe it or not. I'd like to have successful records, but that's it. And I'd very much like never to do any more interviews or anything.

Roger Daltrey: If I wasn't with a group I don't know what I'd do. It means everything to me. I think I'd do myself in.

Roger Daltrey: Look at me. I'm a funny little geezer, really. Skinny. Only five feet seven inches. Bow legs and a lopsided walk. But I was born with star presence. That's an indefinable quality, but I've got it.

Keith Moon: I never considered not being successful.

Pete Townshend: When you're a snotty-nosed kid you suffer from two things. One is an inferiority complex and the other thing is an excessive fantasy. So my inferiority complex said I was never going to get anywhere or do anything, but in dreamland I always imagined that The

Who were going to be the biggest group in the world.

Pete Townshend: When I started off, the object was to make as much money as possible in the shortest time, don't let any fucker get in my way, be a big star, fuck a lot of women, and end up with a mansion in the country. It's taken a lot longer than I thought, and in the meantime I've learnt some sense.

Pete Townshend: Before The Who got big, I wanted them to get bigger and bigger and bigger and bigger until a number one record and then wrap dynamite around their heads and blow them up on TV.

Pete Townshend: The kind of people I admire are those who don't give a monkey's for fame or success. I think the greatest triumph of success is to get there, realise it's no different from the place you started and just try to carry on as though it were normal.

Pete Townshend: I wasn't an adolescent when I was writing stuff like 'I Can't Explain' – it was aimed *at* them, but I was a rock bloke, I was in a band. But then in that situation you stay young — get drunk, smash hotel rooms, be naughty, get into trouble, smash guitars, throw fits — and you get away with it. But there comes a point in your life when you don't want to do that anymore. If everyone was allowed to behave like that for as long as they wanted to, I think they'd behave like that up until now, until the time they were about thirty, and then they'd slow down.

Pete Townshend: All the atrocities of war, why are they created? Why do men spear babies on bayonets? Why do they do it? Because they're not normal, they're not living normal life. When I see rock and roll being guilty of that, you know, that hurts.

Pete Townshend: John is practically unchanged. He always knew where he was going and what he wanted. The girl he would marry was the one he did marry. His only outside influence was Duane Eddy and is Duane Eddy. He's like a rock — but he's a bit of a drinker, especially if it's other people's drink. The fact that he gets less attention than the rest of us might worry him to a degree, but he would never take action. He's come in a straight line from the early days to now.

God.

Pete Townshend: The Christian Church is going into decline and there's a fantastic amount of drug use among the young, most of it leading to a sort of spiritual desperation. People want information of a spiritual nature since we're in a scientific age, but they want facts in a glamorous sort of way. The only thing that can ever do

this is the myth and excitement of a person. If someone says to you "How do I find God?" and you say "Just keep on doing what you're doing," that would really make them angry. They want to know what book to read, where to meditate and that sort of thing. Baba didn't talk about meditation and maybe wouldn't have advocated an album like this (Townshend's solo album 'Who Came First') that doesn't specifically say what he was all about. But he did say it was important for people to hear his name, because at this time he's the highest possible manifestation in human form of Consciousness. He's the highest most advanced soul in the Universe. You can take that with a pinch of salt, but I believe it.

Roger Daltrey, asked if he believes in God: Oh yes. But that's got bugger all to do with the Church. The Church to me is just a big business organisation. Its money should be used to help old age pensioners because they're the most insecure of all. If I had an animal like Lord Longford I'd put him down. Who the fuck do they think they are? Telling us what we should see — and what we shouldn't. When it comes to that — something that really doesn't harm anybody. I just don't believe in censorship. Not necessarily in public, but if you want to buy something or you want to buy a pornographic film to show in your own household. I've bought them before. They're hysterically funny. When you get a bit bored with the missus, they do a lot of good things for you.

Pete Townshend: I'd like to think what I'm working toward is the expression of my genius, believing that everyone is a genius and every man is an expression of the universal consciousness. Every man is an expression of God, every man retains genius and yet the cameo of each person is his ability to communicate his genius to others and let them know what they're at.

Pete Townshend: On a basic working level, songs like 'I'm Free', 'Pinball Wizard' and a couple of others are very much Baba, songs of the quiet explosion of divinity. They just rolled off the pen. But I don't mean divinely inspired! You get a lot of crap from the close devotees of Baba, stories about people rushing up to him and saying "My daughter was dying in Poona and I said a prayer to you and you came in a vision and she was well again." Baba says, "I'm sorry, mate, I don't know anything about that." It's obviously their faith, their love for him that did the trick. It's like Jesus saying, "It's your faith that made you whole."

Pete Townshend: Rama Krishna, Buddha, Zarathustra, Jesus and Meher Baba are all divine figures on earth. They all said the same thing; yet we still trundle on. This is basically what 'Tommy' is saying. But his followers ask how to follow

him, and disregard his teaching. They want rules and regulations — going to church on Sundays — but he just says "Live life". Later he smashes rules to them.

Pete Townshend: It's very weird to be in a group like The Who and feel that you're at a totally different stage of spiritual evolution from the others, and yet at the same stage of physical evolution. We're all very similar as physical bodies, we enjoy the same degree of self-punishment, the same music, we enjoy playing together and so on, but we have different basic ethics of how to live our lives and they don't cross. Deeply written in Who philosophy is the fact that each member thinks the other guy's way is total bullshit but it's all-right-by-me. I may be putting words in people's mouths, but that's probably true. So let's say I'm tolerated in my mystical beliefs, although I should imagine there's a bit of fear in the group that I might grow my hair down my back and start putting out solo albums about . . . do a George Harrison basically. I don't think there's any danger of that because I would never broach the subject of self-awareness as close to my work as Harrison does. A prime example is Inayat Khan who wrote the Sufi literature, started the Sufi indoctrination in the States, and was also a master musician who played the vina. He was *the* bloody master musician. When you went to one of his concerts, you were taken out of your body. I mean that's literally what happened, ridden and riddled and taken out of your ego and removed from yourself and GOD, GOD, GOD. Well he stopped and just started to teach, but he never tried to teach or preach while he was a musician. He stopped being a musician and then went on to preach and teach. I don't think I've ever heard a man who's spoken more truth to me than Dylan, but he's never preached in a song and yet I'm sure he's got a lot of good sense that he could lay on me. I'm not knocking Harrison incidentally 'cause he's a sincere guy.

Pete Townshend, asked if Meher Baba has affected his writing?: Well, the effect has become very clear. I mean, 'Tommy' has got a mystical thread flowing through it, and it's about the spiritual evolution of a man rather than about the sub-teenage frustrations I used to write about before. But most of all it's affected my writing by changing me as an individual, by making me less panicky and more committed to living my life minute to minute. Previous to being involved with Baba I tended to weigh things up very carefully whereas now I'm much more impulsive, I just sort of chase my Karma around with the feeling that Baba's got his thumb on my head, so everything's all right. At the same time I haven't changed all that much. I've still got a bad temper and I'm fairly aggressive as a musician.

MEHER BABA

Quite simply, I write more honestly now. I'm not afraid to write about what I'm thinking, despite the fact that in a case like 'The Seeker' it made quite an embarrassing record. 'The Seeker' had nothing to do with Baba lovers, or Krishna devotees, or whatever. It was a song glorifying the ordinary man in the street who's like hitting people with bottles but still, believe it or not, looking for god realisation even though he doesn't know it. And I found that very amusing and wrote a song about it.

Pete Townshend, on visiting Baba's tomb in India: I really felt like a speck of dust. It was fantastic. Suddenly everything was in proportion. It only lasted three seconds. I yearn to reach that state of excitement and absolute pure peace again.

Pete Townshend: I was worried that I might do more harm than good by announcing my belief. But now in America Baba is fast becoming such a well-known figure that really it was only reinforcement . . . Baba stands on his own. It is not a flirtation like the Maharishi thing. It is something you cannot take lightly. The first thing is to accept that he was either the Messiah or not. If you want more proof after that you have to look for affirmation . . . in retrospect I needed something in my life, but at that time I was not aware of the need. It was not something I went into because I was ruined by drugs or anything. I was in good shape as it happens. But although I was not obsessed by acid it had opened my mind in many ways . . . Ronnie Lane of The Faces is also a follower and he is very matter-of-fact about the

whole thing. I am more interested in these more practical followers than any rituals . . . I can't preach anything — it might be good for you or for anybody else, but they have to find out for themselves.

Punk.

Pete Townshend: Well I reckon it is a deeper commitment to those immortal words "Hope I

die before I get old" which I've had great difficulty living with and growing up with. They have jumped in a bit deeper and have not just said, "Hope I die before I grow old," but they've actually called themselves something which literally limits them to a three-year career.

Pete Townshend: The Who, despite the fact that we do go on and on and on, one of the things that

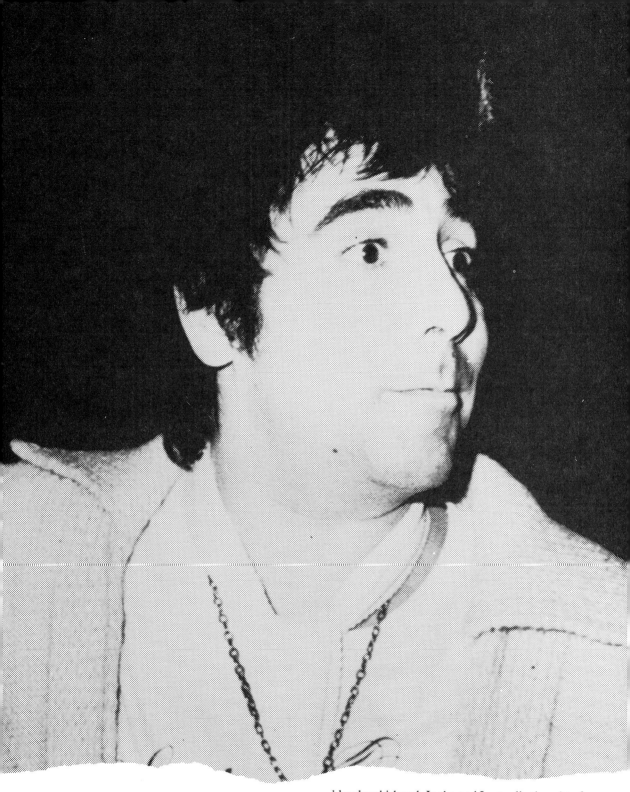

has driven us on and on and on is that we've looked around and said, "Well who is there to pick up the glove?" Nobody. And now there is. And now I think you will find The Who will diversify far more.

Pete Townshend: I used to wake up in the night praying to be destroyed. Get me out of this bloody whirlpool. In the end I actually thought of inventing a new form of music which would take over from where The Who left off. In my imagination I invented punk a thousand times. I thought the hypocrisy of the position we were in was just unbelievable. "Where are the young people of today?" I thought. "Where are their heroes of today?"

Fussin' and Fightin'

Artistic Differences.

Roger Daltrey: Pete's got a bit of a chip because Moony and I used to get all the birds whereas he, as the writer, was the most creative and probably thought he should have all the attention.

Keith Moon: We used to fight regularly. I left the band about three weeks after I joined. I left for about three or four days, though. John and I used to have fights. It wasn't very serious. It was more of an emotional spur-of-the-moment thing.

Pete Townshend: We get on badly. Roger causes a lot of trouble because he is never satisfied with the sound and he is the only one who will speak about it. Roger is not a very good singer at all in my opinion. He has got a good act, but I think he expects a backing group more than an integrated group. I don't think he will ever understand he will never get a backing group.

John Entwistle: During one of the five or so times that The Who has broken up — before we actually turned a profit with 'Tommy' — Keith and I decided we'd go off and form a band with Richard Cole, who used to be our chauffeur. I said, okay, I'm forming this band, and I've got everything all together. I'm gonna write all the stuff and Keith's gonna play drums and we're gonna be a big band — making much more money than The Who would ever make. I was gonna call the band Led Zeppelin and I had

designed a cover of an R/101 Zeppelin going down in flames and I was gonna do it in black and white — very subtle. Two weeks later, Richard Cole went to work for Jimmy Page and you see where our Zeppelin went. The name came from England — in our area the local bands used to meet at the local bar after our gigs and we'd ask, "How'd you go over tonight?" We'd say, "We all went down like a lead zeppelin." So that's where that name came from, then. I was always better at naming groups and designing album covers.

Roger Daltrey: We're never really The Who in the studio. That's one of the difficulties getting records made with the band. There was a lot wrong, but we rectified it on this album ('The Who By Numbers'). We all got stuck in and made a record. But there's not a lot of room for a group because it's becoming more and more dominated by Pete. It's very hard to make a group contribution outside of what you actually do in the band. Outside of me just singing for instance. John seems to do all right at it, but every suggestion *I* make I just get laughed at. But I can live with that. I don't care if I'm just the singer anyway.

Pete Townshend: The production of our records has got nothing to do with sound. It's got to do with trying to keep Keith Moon on his fucking drum stool and keep him away from the booze. And through that period ('Tommy' and just after) it was to do with keeping me from fucking out on some kind of other dope. There was a whole period when Kit Lambert was just keeping us from really fighting. We're a dreadful group to record.

Roger Daltrey: I don't want to be in a group with anybody else, although if I could choose three friends to go about with it wouldn't be those three.

Roger Daltrey: We used to fight a lot — we used to physically fight on stage. I used to call Townshend a cunt and he'd call me a git and he'd hit me with a guitar and I'd be banging him with my microphone and we'd think, "Christ, that's a good sound." Really. That's basically how it started, by literally losing our tempers with each other and taking it out on our instruments.

Roger Daltrey: I've only ever had one fight with Pete and that was during 'Quadrophenia'. It was a bit of a shame because it was a non-argument and the last thing I wanted to do in the world was have a fist fight with Pete Townshend. Unfortunately he hit me first with a guitar. I really felt terrible about it afterwards. What can you say? Pete should never try and be a fighter. But when he was being held back by two roadies and he's spitting at me, calling me a dirty little cunt and

KEITH MOON AT CHARLTON

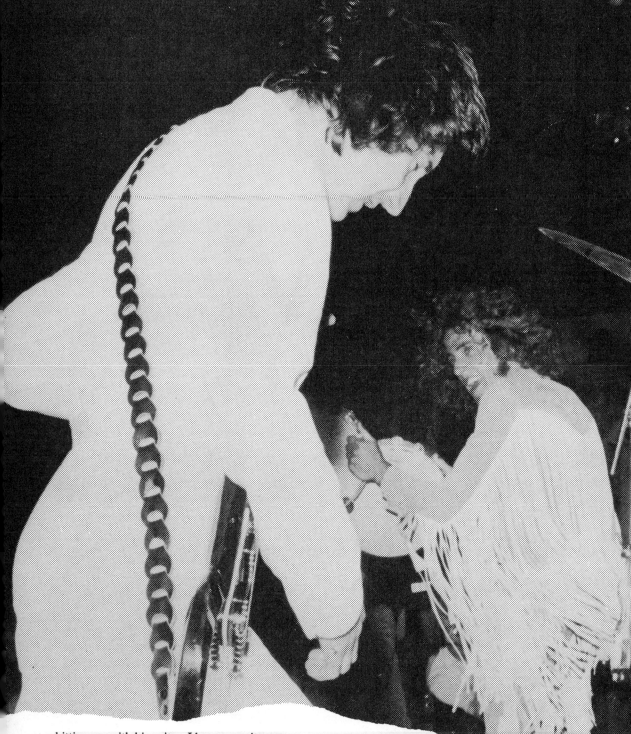

hitting me with his guitar, I became quite angry. And I was forced to lay one on him. But only one.

Roger Daltrey: I've always felt a bit of a misfit with The Who.

Roger Daltrey: We've never had a lot of violence at concerts and things-ever. Because we do it all for them.

Roger Daltrey, on why he fought with Townshend: I didn't like him. He'd have an idea I didn't agree with. I'd have an idea he didn't agree with. I mean, it was just like kids playing games.

Roger Daltrey, on Pete Townshend: He's a very intelligent guy. He's got great perception. But I don't think he's a genius. He's a very good songwriter, one of the best, but it's not good songs alone that go to make The Who. Because I can't consider it intellectually like — intellectual journalists find it difficult to understand what sort

of a contribution someone like me makes to The Who. Rock came from the gutter and still fucking belongs there as far as I'm concerned. I think the beauty of rock is that it is the mood of the people. It's the speech of the kind of people that's in it.

Roger Daltrey: Why do we get on together? Well, in our stars we have the four elements — earth, fire, air and water. Maybe that's got something to do with it.

Roger Daltrey: The Who have always hated me fucking guts, mate. Always. Never been any different. I think it's a deep beneath the surface thing. I mean I lived the first four years after 'My Generation' in perpetual fear of getting kicked out of the band. They didn't want me in it. To me The Who was worth everything. So I just shut up and was very quiet for four years. I think Townshend's always wanted to be me.

Pete Townshend: Roger could be such an easy bloke to dislike. I've disliked him half the time

117

I've been involved with him, and I think maybe for a lot of years he's disliked me or been afraid of me in a funny way.

Keith Moon: Even if The Who split up some day, we'd still be The Who, if you know what I mean.

Pete Townshend, on whether the personal relationships between members of the band have changed from the early "hate each other" days: It exists — remnants of it exist very slightly. When we've all had too much to drink. As you know, a drunken man is a younger man, or thinks he is. And I think we all revert back to childhood a little bit. We were kids, really. The great thing about rock, or the great positive thing about this aspect of rock, is that it does make you feel very young. I'll be thirty next year and it allows me to go onstage and prance around like a lunatic and feel very young, but it also makes you believe you're young and irresponsible, so you end up doing things like smashing hotel rooms and wondering why you're ending up in jail. Originally the group was run by the iron glove of Roger Daltrey. Roger just isn't like he was any more. And hasn't been for years and years. He used to be very tough and liked to get his own way, and if he didn't he'd shout and scream and stamp and in the end he'd punch you in the mouth. We'd all got big egos in the group and none of us liked it, and I think about half way

through the first year we all — John, Keith and I — got together and politely asked Roger to leave.

John Entwistle: I suppose in a way it's treating the band like a marriage — you have arguments but it doesn't mean you should break up. Some bands have an argument and think it's the end of the world — we're not suited, let's split the band up. You've got to treat it like a marriage. You have the arguments, but you've always got to make up.

Pete Townshend: I felt the situation between Roger and me was irredeemable. The things I said I genuinely meant at the time. The reason they got up his nose and why what he said in reply got up my nose was because we were both speaking the truth about one another. We both made it clear we hated one another's guts. And you only hate somebody if you don't know them. I really feel the reverse now. Now if I was gonna pick three friends, I'd *start* with those three. Everybody's changed in the band in the last three years. I think 'By Numbers' was partly responsible for that. But the one thing that's been played down like mad — because it's very painful for the band to talk about — is that we're going through litigation with our management, Kit Lambert and Chris Stamp; people we loved. I felt myself being pulled in two different directions, and in the end I had to let go my friendship with Kit and Chris and run with the band. [1978]

Join Together In The Band.

KEITH MOON, 1972

Onstage.

Keith Moon: It's not a question of one person trying to upstage the other, for we're all in it together. If one of us can see whatever it is the audience needs at that particular moment, to get them up and going, then that person does it. Onstage we're part of the audience and they're part of us.

Keith Moon: I wouldn't have joined the band if I didn't think they were magnificent. If I thought there was a better group I'd do my best to play with 'em. But there isn't.

John Entwistle: The reason we've lasted so long is because when we go on stage we all try to upstage one another. We play full tilt from the very start. Then, at the end of each set we have to pull something extra out of the bag as a climax. Really, it's as simple as that. Likewise, if we kept quiet and didn't jibe at each other in interviews, then The Who would no longer exist. Another reason why we've lasted so long is simply because we recognise each other's faults.

Keith Moon: Anytime is the best time with The Who. Onstage looking at each other working is the best time. Just when you're flat out and everybody is doing their job best. When we look at each other and smile and exchange glances on stage, and we're cooking. Yeah, that's the best time. The Who is more than everything to me. Everything plus. There's nothing corny about love, and I love The Who.

121

John Entwistle: The story about me being the quiet one of The Who is not quite true. Roger is the hermit. When we're on tour, we never see him except on stage.

Keith Moon: I couldn't have stood ten years with one band, but spending ten years or ten minutes with The Who is like spending a lifetime with a hundred different groups.

Pete Townshend: I've never ever gone on and done that showbusiness thing. Roger does. Roger can go on and act – he's got tremendous presence, which

he switches on and off like a light bulb. He walks on that fucking stage and he's like a magnet. It's a spine chilling procedure.

Pete Townshend: Sometimes, during the depths of a really bad day, I really would like to crawl off and die, but I realise that there's something very magical about being on stage and part of a band that's working together. It's very fulfilling because it's always been kinda dangerous and risky and that's what rock has always thrived on — risk.

The Audience.

Keith Moon: They just stand there looking thick in their knitted woollen jumpers which is all they can get. And they say to us, "You're queer." And I say to them "Come back to the hotel."

Pete Townshend: Sometimes you feel like attacking them. You will just be getting really musically involved and some stupid girl with FREDDIE tattooed on her front will come up and cry, "Ringo." You feel like smashing her with Coke bottles.

Pete Townshend: When you've got an audience it is one of the most exhilarating experiences you can have, like dropping your trousers in front of the people. It's *the* exhibitionist's delight, to do something really big in front of people. Okay, they know you're going to go out there and sing and play, so it becomes nothing. For the first couple of years that's great, but then you want more. You want people to tear their hair out when you appear, and when they don't you feel you've got to extend your end a bit; you've really got to make them spew up. I think a lot of groups are just now [1967] finding out what audiences

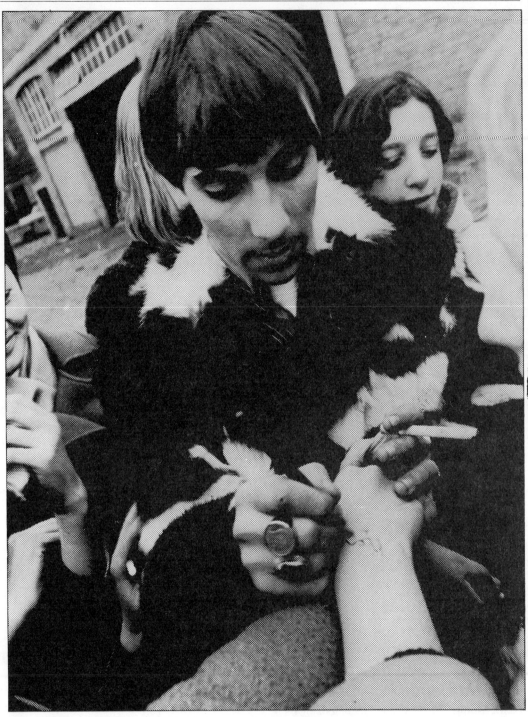

want. This is probably why acid's popular — because it makes you part of the audience. You take it, you sit back, there's no work, and off you go. It's twenty-four hours of touring. I think everyone's a member of an audience, everyone wants to sit back and watch.

Roger Daltrey: I think our fans are one of the biggest reasons for us staying together. I think

we've got the most sincere lot for a rock audience that you could ever wish to have.

Pete Townshend: The really great thing about rock and roll is that it's a communication between people that're in glass houses. They're all enshrouded in their own secret worlds, they can't break out, but they can talk to each other through rock and roll. A kid'll come up and say,

"You said exactly what I felt then!" and of course he could have told somebody or I could have, but it's done in this oblique way, and it's such an invigorating process to know that this release is happening. Then you get to a rock concert, and that song — say 'My Generation' — about frustration, about feeling so rotten and out of it that you resort to dope, about feeling so frustrated with older people that you despise them so much you never want to be like them in any way whatsoever . . . feelings that you've never been able to express clearly — is what everyone around you is applauding and you know they feel the same way as you do.

Roger Daltrey: I think 'See Me Feel Me' will always be in our act. You know the words are

really true. It's through them (the audience) that we hear the music — through them that we progress.

Pete Townshend: Some kid writes to me and says, "I've got all your records and I listen to your music all day long and I look at your pictures all the time and I write to you and all I get is a bleedin' autographed picture. You don't know how much time I spend thinkin' about you lot." I write back to him and say, "You don't know how much time I spend looking at and thinking about teenagers."

Pete Townshend: In fact, sometimes I really do believe that we're the only rock band on the face of this planet that knows what rock and roll is all about.